LOW-INCOME FEMALE TEACHER VALUES AND AGENCY IN INDIA

Key Issues in Social Justice: Voices from the Frontline

Series Editors: Kalwant Bhopal, University of Birmingham, **Martin Myers**, Universirty of Nottingham, **Karl Kitching**, University of Birmingham and **Kenzo Sung**, Rowan University

---

How do issues of social justice, inclusion and equity shape modern day society? This series delivers a forum for perspectives from historically marginalised and minoritised communities to challenge contemporary dominant discourses about social justice, inclusion and equity in the social sciences and aligned disciplines.

Also available

Transformative Teaching and Learning in Further Education: Pedagogies of Hope and Social Justice
By **Rob Smith and Vicky Duckworth**

Hidden Voices: Lived Experiences in the Irish Welfare Space
By **Joe Whelan**

Forthcoming

Permanent Racism: Race, Class and the Myth of Post-racial Britain
By **Paul Warmington**

Disrupting the Academy with Lived Experience-Led Knowledge
Edited by **Maree Higgins** and **Caroline Lenette**

Find out more

policy.bristoluniversitypress.co.uk/
key-issues-in-social-justice

LOW-INCOME FEMALE TEACHER VALUES AND AGENCY IN INDIA
Implications for Reflective Practice

Ruth Samuel

First published in Great Britain in 2025 by

Policy Press, an imprint of
Bristol University Press
University of Bristol
1–9 Old Park Hill
Bristol
BS2 8BB
UK
t: +44 (0)117 374 6645
e: bup-info@bristol.ac.uk

Details of international sales and distribution partners are available at
policy.bristoluniversitypress.co.uk

© Bristol University Press 2025

British Library Cataloguing in Publication Data
A catalogue record for this book is available from the British Library

ISBN 978-1-4473-6097-1 hardcover
ISBN 978-1-4473-6098-8 paperback
ISBN 978-1-4473-6099-5 ePub
ISBN 978-1-4473-6100-8 ePdf

The right of Ruth Samuel to be identified as author of this work has been asserted by her in accordance with the Copyright, Designs and Patents Act 1988.

All rights reserved: no part of this publication may be reproduced, stored in a retrieval system, or transmitted in any form or by any means, electronic, mechanical, photocopying, recording, or otherwise without the prior permission of Bristol University Press.

Every reasonable effort has been made to obtain permission to reproduce copyrighted material. If, however, anyone knows of an oversight, please contact the publisher.

The statements and opinions contained within this publication are solely those of the author and not of the University of Bristol or Bristol University Press. The University of Bristol and Bristol University Press disclaim responsibility for any injury to persons or property resulting from any material published in this publication.

Bristol University Press and Policy Press work to counter discrimination on grounds of gender, race, disability, age and sexuality.

Cover design: Liam Roberts Design
Front cover image: iStock/amlanmathur

Bristol University Press' authorised representative in the European Union is:
Easy Access System Europe, Mustamäe tee 50, 10621 Tallinn, Estonia,
Email: gpsr.requests@easproject.com

Contents

Series editor's preface — vi
List of figures and tables — viii
Acknowledgements — x
Preface — xi

1 Positioning female teachers in the context of India — 1
2 Teachers' perceptions of their roles — 29
3 Teachers' perspectives on navigating social spaces — 67
4 Teachers' attitudes to transformation — 101
5 Conclusion — 125

References — 147
Index — 156

Series editor's preface

Kalwant Bhopal

Debates about social justice, inclusion and equity in the early 21st century have become increasingly more contentious and problematic. This should not come as a surprise and reflects Western social, economic and political climates driven by neoliberal narratives; the rapid expansion of European Union membership, followed by signs of its impending potential dissolution; the election of Donald Trump as 45th president of the United States in 2016; and the growing populism of nationalist political parties in almost every Western democracy. At the same time, the Global South has seen economic expansion on a scale undreamt of a generation ago that threatens to undermine the hegemony of the West.

This original book series delivers a forum for marginalised and minoritised perspectives in the social sciences. It challenges contemporary dominant discourses about social justice, inclusion and equity from the perspective of marginalised and minoritised communities. Drawing upon the work of researchers, theorists and practitioners from Europe, the US and the Global South, the series adopts a broad interdisciplinary approach, including disciplines such as education, sociology, social policy and childhood studies. The titles in the series are published on broad topics, underpinned by research and theory.

The series draws upon definitions of social justice that identify the marginalisation and exclusion of groups and communities of people based on their difference from the majority population. The series seeks to understand how such processes should be disrupted and subverted. Social justice in this respect is not only the subject matter of the book series but also its practical contribution to academic scholarship. By providing an outlet for scholarship that itself emerges from underrepresented voices, the books published in the series contribute to addressing rather than simply commenting on social justice issues. The series centres social justice, inclusion and equity as a key focus; gives voice to those from marginalised communities and groups; places a spotlight on the work of underrepresented (minority ethnic, religious, disabled, female, LGBTQ) academics; and challenges hegemonic narratives that underpin Western discourses about how best to reach a socially just world.

A key strength of the series includes a broad range of topics from different disciplines in the social sciences, including education, sociology, social policy, gender studies, migration and international relations, politics and childhood studies. The series draws on themes which include race/ethnicity, gender, class, sexuality, age, poverty, disability and other topics which address and challenge inequalities. It includes a range of different theoretical perspectives, including addressing intersectional identities.

Low-income Female Teacher Values and Agency in India explores how teachers on low incomes in Bangalore express their values within the school context. The book focuses on three themes: the social relationships between teachers and students, how teachers define their social spaces, and how the school can be used as a transformative space for teachers and their students. Drawing on interviews with teachers, Samuel provides us with rich, important engaging data to demonstrate how respondents are able to use their voice and exercise agency to instigate change in the classroom. Samuel powerfully explodes the myth that women in Indian society are marginalised; instead, she demonstrates how her respondents are acutely aware of their environment and are able to exert forms of social control and negotiate their social spaces in their teaching. This book provides an original contribution to analysing gender and education within the Indian context and reminds us of the importance of understanding how the classroom can be a space for female teachers' empowerment.

List of figures and tables

Figures

0.1	Book chapter outline	xii
1.1	Chapter 1 outline	1
1.2	NEP 2020, length of study and options for prior degrees	15
1.3	Research design with individual and group interviews	27
2.1	Chapter 2 outline	29
2.2	Social relationship between teacher and student mediated by performance	39
3.1	Chapter 3 outline	67
3.2	Outline of mixed/multi-method approach and data analysis tools of inquiry development	69
3.3	Key elements of maintaining peace of mind based on responses	81
3.4	Division of internal and external social spaces in relation to external conflict and teachers' productive internal space with their students	86
3.5	Space for agency to occur between internal language (Kannada) and external form of communication (English language)	90
4.1	Chapter 4 outline	101
4.2	Habermas's development of authentic knowledge and social praxis	107
4.3	Low-income female teachers' social praxis as defined by responses	108
4.4	Distributed personhood of knowledge and authority within the Indian classroom	120
5.1	Chapter 5 outline	125
5.2	Agency within teacher roles, social spaces and attitudes to transformation	126
5.3	The classroom as a space for female teacher agency	129
5.4	Explicit and visible agency through speech, as defined by negotiating between different expectations and roles	140

Tables

1.1	Overview of distribution across interviews, observations and group discussion	28
2.1	Teachers' perceptions of their role in relation to reflective practice in teacher education	64

List of figures and tables

3.1	Detail from syntax intonation data analysis matrix (a)	70
3.2	Detail from syntax intonation data analysis matrix (b)	71
3.3	Teachers' perspectives on navigating social spaces in relation to reflective practice	100
4.1	Teachers' attitudes to transformation in relation to reflective practice	102
5.1	Teacher effectiveness to support female teacher agency	143

Acknowledgements

I would like to acknowledge my parents, Rev Vinay Kumar Samuel and Mrs Colleen Samuel, for the values they have instilled within me, through their lifelong commitment to transformation for marginalised communities in Bangalore and across the world.

It is the compassion and deep insight of my mother, Colleen, that have driven my research and personal commitment to our community in Lingarajapuram, Bangalore. Her vision that no child is left behind in their education and opportunities to fulfil their dreams is one that I share and strive to maintain. My father Vinay's invaluable advice provided the ultimate support during my research and in writing up this book. His vast knowledge and work in transformation and development globally provided an irreplaceable foundation to my academic and personal development.

Finally, and most importantly, I would like to thank my wonderful husband, Neil D'Monte for his unwavering support and encouragement. Sacrifices made by him enabled me to research, write and gain strength along the way.

Preface

This book examines the implications of teacher values on female teacher agency and how this can support reflective practice within teacher education in India.

I aim to share new research, as well as to highlight the need for education research in India to include individual and idiosyncratic data. Research that highlights life histories and the varied experiences of Indian teachers can greatly support reflective practice within pre- and in-service teacher training. It can emphasise the feminine perspective within educational development, especially the impact of the social and cultural contexts within which the individual low-income female teacher lives.

This book will focus on distinct ways teachers enacted agency through their speech when participating in interviews. Teachers were careful and selective about the way they spoke to me when responding to questions. The way they constructed and reconstructed their speech revealed their unique skill in using the English language to defend, protect or define how they were to be perceived. Although this may be expected of any participant being interviewed, it was particularly interesting how teachers' speech aligned with or, at times, contradicted their views. How teachers speak helps to understand how they view their relationships, how they are represented, and what they think of their teaching practice. Within a strong oral tradition in India, the teacher's voice in my research proved to be a crucial resource in which female agency, freedom and empowerment were enacted.

The primacy given in this book to the teacher's voice and its skilful use contests a perception of low-income women in India as being unable to speak for themselves and exercise agency. Indeed, women in India are distinctly marginalised, their freedoms are socially and culturally restricted, and these issues persist. However, their marginalised status does not mean they are helpless in how they are represented. I put forward that low-income female teachers are acutely aware of their environment and careful negotiators of their social spaces. They are aware of how they are perceived and exert forms of control over such perceptions through their speech and voice.

Although specific to the Indian context, the themes and focus of this book can help us understand how embedded social actors operate. The complex relationship between female teacher values and implications for reflective practice in India outlines the entangled nature of agency, freedom and voice within wider contexts of gender and teacher identity in the Global South.

Chapter outline

As background to responses by the teachers interviewed, Chapter 1 sets out ways in which female teachers are marginalised and continually displaced (see Figure 0.1). Social, economic and education contexts of female teacher displacement examine restrictions placed on women's work and income levels, educational opportunities for girls and their role within the household, as well as the impact of educational culture and policy on the teacher's role. Chapter 1 concludes with an argument for taking account of the lived experiences of low-income female teachers as a response to their lack of representation within policy and education development within India.

Chapters 2, 3 and 4 focus on teacher responses within individual and group interviews as well as lesson observations. These are divided into the three main values into which teacher responses were grouped. Key areas of methodology are outlined across Chapters 2, 3 and 4 and provide a framework for the analysis of teacher responses and themes discussed within each chapter.

Chapter 2 outlines teacher's perceptions of their roles. This includes their social relationships with students and colleagues, expectations of student behaviour, dynamics of the classroom and motivations to become a teacher. Family expectations and roles are also examined in Chapter 2, as this provides a crucial foundation for understanding

Figure 0.1: Book chapter outline

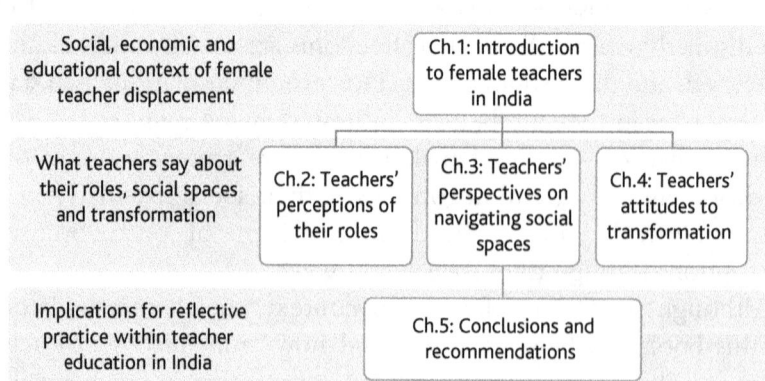

why women from low-income backgrounds choose to teach and how this contributes to their need to stay within the profession.

Chapter 3 examines the way teachers defined their social spaces in terms of who was part of their community and who was outside this. The definition of community itself is explored in this chapter, in relation to teacher relationships that maintain social cohesion by avoiding internal conflict and protecting each other from external intrusion. This chapter also builds on teachers' understanding of core neoliberal ideologies that have defined education policy in India, by commenting on what a meaningful life is for themselves.

Chapter 4 centres upon teachers' understanding of Habermas's notion of authentic knowledge and what they believe is transformation for their students and themselves. This chapter draws upon teacher responses so as to examine their social praxis as defined by a form of distributed personhood to pass on knowledge to their students.

Chapter 5 brings together key areas discussed in Chapters 2, 3 and 4 to focus on what they can tell us about female teacher agency. This discussion contributes to outlining recommendations to support effective reflective practice among teachers in India. Teacher values outlined in previous chapters act as the foundation for understanding female teacher agency and how reflective practice can be developed within teacher education. Specifically, Chapter 5 outlines the classroom as a space for female teacher empowerment and how reworking teacher effectiveness in India can support reflective practice.

1

Positioning female teachers in the context of India

This chapter provides an overview of the social and educational context within which female teachers in India operate (see Figure 1.1). A key theme is the degree to which they are displaced within Indian society through social and economic marginalisation, as well as the impact of education culture and policy on their role and status within and outside the classroom. Examining how women are displaced can help us to understand the conditions under which low-income female teachers negotiate and navigate their values and agency within their professional and personal lives. Recent policy on teacher education made through the National Education Policy (NEP, 2020) and future implications for low-income female teachers are covered. The chapter concludes with an argument for the lived experiences of low-income female teachers in India to be taken into account to respond to their continued marginalisation within Indian society and the education system.

Social and economic displacement of female teachers

Women's work and income in India

Cultural and historical inequalities within India have led to contexts in which women for the most part negotiate their education, choices and

Figure 1.1: Chapter 1 outline

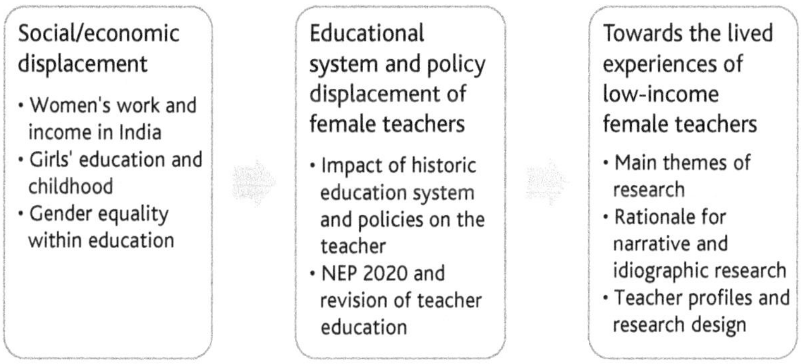

Social/economic displacement	Educational system and policy displacement of female teachers	Towards the lived experiences of low-income female teachers
• Women's work and income in India • Girls' education and childhood • Gender equality within education	• Impact of historic education system and policies on the teacher • NEP 2020 and revision of teacher education	• Main themes of research • Rationale for narrative and idiographic research • Teacher profiles and research design

earning capacity across different strata of society (Basu, 2010; Busby, 1999; Maslak and Singhal, 2008; Manjrekar, 2013; Sanghani, 2015). Marriage is a key area in which female marginalisation takes place, with obligation to family passed from parents to the husband's family. Marriage impacts on women's choice of job, if they are allowed to work, including family responsibilities in taking care of their husband, their children and their husband's family. Maslak and Singhal (2008) found that Indian women with a higher education degree defined themselves through being a mother, wife and daughter-in-law when deciding to pursue professional positions. College-educated, middle-class women navigated between different social, cultural and religious obligations when planning their professional development. The study called for a greater understanding of the complexities of family obligation faced by women when deciding upon social and economic policy strategy.

For low-income women, these complexities are even greater as they lack financial resources, education and social status afforded to middle-class women. Low-income female contribution to family, even though financially equal to that of their husband, is mediated by a subordinate position within the family. Research studies examining the lives of lower social status women, mainly those with low literacy, (Busby, 1999; Chaturvedi et al, 2009) outlined the prevalence of social and family obligations. Lower-income women adopted a belief in negotiable fate to cope with a lack of direct control over their lives and subjugation to external forces whether social, economic, or spousal, including spousal violence and abuse.

Busby (1999) examined routine domestic violence perpetrated by fishermen in Kerala on their wives, which was seen as part of married life. Division of labour within the fishing community meant men ventured out to sea with their wives selling their catch and managing their household income. According to Busby, the appearance of equality in terms of labour and roles is contrasted with widespread domestic violence. Busby sees this as supported by an understanding of a woman's place in society and especially in relation to her husband. Lower incomes necessitate that women need to work and contribute to the family income, sharing what is traditionally a man's role as provider. Violence and spousal abuse maintain the women's subordinate role within the marriage and within their communities. The woman may work and contribute equally but she is still beaten and abused to maintain the husband's position within and outside the household.

Women in India generally lack control over their income (Ramachandran, 2000, 2003). Women's work is to look after the family or labour in the agricultural field and is considered to have little or no monetary value. The core of female powerlessness within India, according to Ramachandran, is their vulnerability, which determines their status. The root to this powerlessness lies within the way society is structured to restrict female knowledge and education to food, health, cattle, and agriculture, with further education seen as unnecessary. Women are denied access to ownership of land or commodities as they are themselves part of their father's or spouse's property. They cannot claim ownership of that of which they are a part. The symbolic binding of women to their male protector underlines a commodification of women within Indian society. They maintain and provide for the family with their intangible contributions being part of the expected duties and responsibilities of care and nurture. They do not control or access resources or knowledge beyond these maternal, nurturing functions. Ramachandran breaks these down to notions of access and control. Access indicates the opportunity to use resources such as healthcare or taking out a loan. However control is more complex; it is shared power and ongoing negotiation. Control is negotiating to live a life of dignity as a woman, to reduce one's vulnerability through owning land or resources, and having access to credit self-help groups. Control, however, is not necessarily a shift of decision making from man to woman but one in which the woman negotiates control.

Girls' education and childhood

Education is another area of control, especially in relation to which level of education girls are allowed to study and the subsequent cost. Secondary education is considered sufficient for a girl who is legally allowed to marry and then becomes the property of her husband and his family. Improving access to post-secondary school education enables girls to gain further skills and a route to higher education and skilled labour. This builds their earning capacity and contribution to their family's financial stability outside of their domestic role and value.

Low numbers of girls receiving secondary education in maths and science are attributed by Ramachandran (2000, 2003) to family reluctance to pay higher fees for their daughters. These subjects are considered unnecessary or irrelevant to their education, indicating their role within the family as they grow up.

Kumar (2010, 2011) outlines colonial reluctance within the British Raj to interfere in child marriage and the practice of sati (in which a widowed wife is burned along with her husband on his funeral pyre) as not wanting to engage in cultural practices seen as private and domestic. Child marriage was eventually banned in 1929 through the Sarada Act (Child Marriage Restraint Act), reducing the minimum age of marriage to 14. Kumar states that Indian nationalist debate at the time contributed to the delay in banning child marriage, since they argued that protecting cultural and social practices extended to the Indian female body which was used as a space for resistance against colonial interference.

Nationalist debate against colonial rule was founded in patriarchy that permitted gender inequality and displacement under an argument of colonial resistance. At the heart of this is the notion of childhood and what it means to be female child within Indian society and culture. For girls, childhood stops once they start assisting in domestic duties or looking after their male siblings. With the more favoured status of the boy within the family, the girl learns to place themselves second to their brother within their daily lives. As the girl matures and starts to menstruate, her shame is perpetuated by either removing her physically from the home while she menstruates or disallowing her from preparing food or passing on 'bad luck' to young children. The girl is essentially made to feel guilt and shame for the very functions that make her biologically female. Kumar outlines this self-denial as a form of self-restriction and self-regulation that girls follow from the example of women around them within the household, so that they learn early on what their main role is within the family and therefore within society.

Within a context in which girls and women are marginalised in terms of their access to and control of income and resources, access to education and their status within their family, female teachers occupy a unique space of being salaried workers who do contribute financially to their family. They occupy a profession in which they exert some forms of control over social relationships with their students and demonstrate their subject knowledge.

Gender equality within education in India

For all income groups in India in 2018, 23.6 per cent of women worked compared to almost 79 per cent of men (World Bank, 2019b). Women make up at least 48.5 per cent of the population but make up to a quarter of the labour force. In terms of income level, women on a low income are 64 per cent of all working women compared to 79 per cent of all working men (World Bank, 2019a). Gender-based wage differentials are not indicated in the World Bank data, but it is expected that women earn significantly less than men. This is embedded deep within Indian society and has been the subject of wide-ranging research within social science and anthropology and helped form seminal post-colonial theory, such as Gayatri Spivak's work on the subaltern female (Spivak, 2005).

Teachers in India are classed under the category 'wage and salaried workers' as those who receive a regular income with an oral or written contract. Wage and salaried workers among women are about 18.8 per cent of the labour force rising from 9 per cent to 18.8 per cent over 17 years. In contrast, larger percentages of working women do not receive a regular salaried income, working in agriculture, industry, service, and as contributing family workers (World Bank, 2019a). In Karnataka, 83.5 per cent of schools have at least two or more female teachers working for them, indicating the relative popularity of teaching among female teachers across most schools in the state (Unified District Information System for Education, 2014).

As a low-cost solution for teacher shortages, an increasing number of contract teachers are employed in India; they are paid 20 to 25 per cent of the monthly salary of a government teacher (International Labour Organisation and UNESCO, 2015) and between 14 to 12.5 per cent in private schools, as they tend to be younger, less experienced, female, and less likely to have received pre-service training.

Therefore, the views of a crucial minority of low-income female teachers are important to understand. They are part of 23.6 per cent of the female labour force and work for a fraction of a government teacher's salary yet are part of a large percentage of teachers working in primary and secondary school education.

Ramachandran's (Jandhyala and Ramachandran, 2009) research into the low numbers of female teachers within secondary schools revealed that, within an estimated 8.3 million primary and secondary teachers employed nationally in 2011, female teachers were just over 40 per cent of all secondary school teachers with a higher percentage of 49 per cent in primary schools in 2010 (International Labour Organisation and UNESCO, 2015; Planning Commission Government of India, 2015). Barriers restricting female teachers from teaching science and maths at secondary school indicate a specific marginalisation of the Indian woman. Teacher training for women encourages primary and elementary school training over secondary school training.

This is supported by fears for women's safety within a secondary school co-educational environment, as well as prioritising male teachers teaching more difficult, higher level subjects. Fear for a female teacher's safety glazes over crucial structural inequalities where sexual harassment exists in India to the point of it being endemic, and almost expected. Instead of helping to address some of these inequalities through supporting a woman to be a secondary school science or maths teacher, women are discouraged by fears over their safety. Fundamentally, Ramachandran notes, stressing primary and elementary training for women over secondary school training underlines patriarchal attitudes to girls and women in Indian society.

In response to such deep-rooted inequality for girls within Indian society, subsequent education reforms encouraged girls to study, resulting in a larger number of female workers with access to education. This called for studies to examine the impact of such reforms on how women negotiate both their personal professional roles and responsibilities (Manjrekar, 2013). Manjrekar argues a neoliberal commodification of education has led to women being employed as low-wage teachers, further reducing their capacity to earn and to contribute to their family. Social reproduction, states Manjrekar, ought to be examined in school and within the family, focusing on the personal and professional lives of female teachers. The higher numbers of educated women seeking employment necessitates a greater understanding of their experiences of reform and of the ways they negotiate spaces in which social reproduction takes place, within the school and their home.

Social reproduction and female agency

Social reproduction and female agency among Indian women are a prominent theme within postcolonial literature on the subaltern female. In a return to her seminal work in postcolonial theory, Spivak (Spivak, 2005) outlines her argument against the use of the low-income Indian female (subaltern) for research purposes. She reasserts the subaltern as those that have no examples, are not represented nor part of caste or class, and essentially without identity. Globalisation has left the subaltern permeable and exploited as part of intellectual property without sharing in the benefits from research. Spivak states that unless the subaltern identifies aspects of themselves to form a collective, they will be continually identified through their difference and made popular through their alterity. This is where teacher values, as a form of collective beliefs, can contribute to a deeper understanding of the Indian teacher.

Despite a good deal of literature examining gender and education within India, there is a lack of specific research looking at female teachers and their teaching practice (Manjrekar, 2013). Studies examining teacher–student relationships allude to the teacher as mother (Gupta, 2003; Joshi, 2009), given the high number of women as teachers. The maternal role of the teacher is an accepted aspect of the teacher's interaction with her students and an extension of her own relationship with her children. The teacher, in taking care of another person's child, brings a direct honesty to her interaction. The teacher is free to scold and encourage the student and emotionally invest in her students in ways that would seem at odds with international ideas of professionalism within teaching (Gupta, 2003).

With greater numbers of women accessing education and employment, and the dominance of women in teaching, teacher values in relation to female agency and empowerment need to consider gender from a female perspective. In relation to Spivak (2005), the context of the subordinate woman is not a question of underrepresentation but, where there has been no representation, of how representation must come from the women themselves.

Social and economic displacement of the female teacher builds upon the marginalised status of the girl-child and women in India. Female teachers face barriers to the level at which they can teach; most teach in primary and middle school with mainly male teachers teaching higher rated subjects in secondary school. Girls and women negotiate their earning capacity through their level of education and economic independence with their families and husband. The concept of 'negotiating' is significant, as female teachers who are 'wage and salaried' workers, navigate the contexts in which they are embedded so that they can earn and contribute to their family income beyond a domestic construct. It is important to understand the complex structures in which these teachers live and operate, especially as we examine the impact of education policy on their role within the classroom and access to quality teacher training.

Education system and policy displacement of female teachers
Impact of historic education system and policies on the teacher's role

This section on the impact of the education system and policies on the Indian teacher must start with one of the main symbols of an Indian classroom, the textbook. The textbook is a key signifier of teacher displacement and control by state and central administration. It is also a crucial foundation for this book's focus, as teacher reliance on textbooks typifies a strong summative learning tradition in India, where performing well in exams shows how well a student has imbibed and reproduced textbook material distributed by the teacher. This is discussed further in Chapter 4 as part of understanding how teachers approach authentic knowledge and transformation. How textbooks are used within India, especially among teachers who are not confident in the subject or have received insufficient training, builds on teachers' dependency and use of exams to mark pre-formed answers from the textbook. Kumar's (Kumar, 1988) notable paper on the origins of India's textbook culture argues that colonial education still influences education administration and attitudes towards knowledge and learning today.

The roots of the Indian teacher's reliance on textbooks were established during the colonial era through the East India Company, which introduced a centralised system where syllabi, textbooks and training aimed to acculturate Indians to British culture. A loyal group of colonial administrators used English language as the main way they communicated and exercised their authority. Centralised examinations started by the East India Company are still practised across India today. Candidates were assessed on textbook material and not on theory or problems. Kumar states that this established rote-learning through mechanical memorisation of knowledge in which practical or vocational skills were not included. These examinations focused on literary knowledge where students were examined externally. External centralised examinations helped project colonial rule as fair and impartial through uniform standards for promotion, scholarship and employment which Indian subjects could feel part of and be promoted within. However, centralised exams also maintained social control and promoted a fear of failure among students. Knowledge, memory and ability were combined, leading to knowledge tied to memorising literary material and failure attached to one's inability to memorise and prepare for examinations.

This trend of central control continued in post-independence India; reforms centralised curriculum and texts through the National Council for Education, Research and Training (NCERT), which published textbooks distributed by different states. The quality of textbook production within post-independence was an issue, as content and exercises were often inaccurate and of low quality. Enabling teachers to make informed decisions on materials and curriculum, according to Kumar (1988), can help avoid their reliance on textbooks and help them exercise greater autonomy. The key to change within the classroom is tied to teacher agency and autonomy, yet the context in which the teacher operates works against such autonomy. The teacher is bound to administrative controls that impact their job security, societal and cultural obligations (Clarke, 2001).

The erosion of the teacher's role and sublimation into administrative duties is a strong theme within Indian education research (Singal, 2006; Hodkinson and Devarakonda, 2011; Sriprakash, 2011; Smail, 2013). This was partly brought about by a policy shift towards child-centred education to produce globally performing, independent learners. Teachers would act as facilitators of learning as opposed to traditional disseminators of knowledge.

The Salamanca Statement (UNESCO and Ministry of Education and Science Spain, 1994) put forward child-centred pedagogy and inclusive education as global education policy and law (Singal, 2005, 2006). In response, the Indian government introduced inclusive policies in the Delhi Declaration for Education for All, 1994, and the Persons with Disability Act, 1995 (Singal, 2006) with a central government focus to improve access to education and start policy evaluation research (Hodkinson and Devarakonda, 2011; Sriprakash, 2011; Smail, 2013).

Indian policies reshaped a child-centred model with social transformation intentions. However, there were discrepancies between policy directive and implementation at training and school level (Singal, 2005; Hodkinson and Devarakonda, 2011). Despite using inclusive education practices within their teaching, Indian teachers attributed their effectiveness and success to a rote-education system (Hodkinson and Devarakonda, 2011). The impact of CCP (child-centred policy) on teachers is notable, with research stating it led to a sense of reduced social status among their community as they were removed from being prime actors within the classroom to being facilitators (Sriprakash, 2011; Smail, 2013). This is common across different countries, but within India social relationships are maintained through the continual ritual of contact and communication. The social status of the Indian schoolteacher relies on their direct act of teaching and instruction to enact their authority and knowledge (Joshi and Taylor, 2005; Sriprakash, 2011; Smail, 2013). India's child-centred policies intend to impart agency to the child through the facilitator role of the teacher. However, it is this facilitator role that prevents teachers from developing autonomy or agency for themselves (Kumar, 2010, 2011).

Neoliberal education policies

Kumar (2005, 2010, 2011) states CCP is an example of how education has been commodified through neoliberal emphasis on business and industry protocols, where teaching and learning are aligned with business quality. Teachers are placed within a distinct behaviourist model focused on the predictability of outcomes and measurability. As service providers, they are required to meet quality standards with greater responsibility within the outcome-oriented institutional cultures in which they work. Teachers are left with greater administrative responsibilities that assess their quality and efficiency but result in reduced time spent with students.

The basis of Kumar's statement on the destructive impact of neoliberal education policies in India can be seen in the influence of Amartya Sen's 'human capability paradigm' (Sen, 2005) and Martha Nussbaum's 'central human capabilities' (Nussbaum, 2009). The human development paradigm, or 'capability approach', refocused education as a key factor in social and economic success, pushing a neoliberal agenda of individual achievement within a collective society (Mooij, 2008; Morrow, 2013; Oser, 2013). Nussbaum and Sen are credited with developing a capability ethic (Crocker, 1992; Feldman and Gellert, 2006; Nussbaum, 2007) that introduced a philosophical and conscientious framework to deal with international economic development. The capability approach offered a critique of traditional development approaches that focused on basic needs, such as food, water and shelter, as only meeting minimal levels of sustaining life. For Sen and Nussbaum, re-envisioning needs as capabilities improved upon basic needs as it dealt directly with what a person can do and be. It allows not only for human achievement in health and nourishment but also for literacy and a choice to lead a valued life (Crocker, 1992; Nussbaum, 2009).

Education is a 'valuable functioning' or basic capability, part of a wider initiative involving political participation and improved health care (Crocker, 1992; Sen, 2005; Nussbaum, 2009). Through better education, a better quality of life is enabled, developing a person's productivity, and contributing to their material prosperity (Sen, 1997; Anand and Sen, 2000). Thus, education has an indirect effect or value on a person's capability and economic stability. Improving human capability does not just increase human capital but also moves towards social development.

For marginalised groups, the concept of human capability acknowledges an individual's basic capability to lead a worthwhile life.

If a person receives a better education leading to better employment prospects and increased income, this contributes to their social standing within their community. Education essentially enables economic and social aspirations and extends beyond human capital as commodity production and valuable functioning. Individuals who receive education are better enabled to achieve or enact their desired values, such as wellbeing or happiness.

What of the idea of capability and choice itself? Nussbaum's (1999) list of central human capabilities outlines ten core capabilities to guide international development. These are: being able to live a normal length of life; bodily health, including reproductive health; bodily integrity in terms of security and freedom of movement; senses, imagination and thought to think, reason and have enjoyable experiences with freedom of expression; emotions through love and care; practical reason through critical reflection on the concept of good and liberty of conscience; affiliation in being able to live with others and having social bases of self-respect and non-humiliation; respect for other species; play; and control over one's environment, both political and material.

Two main criticisms with Nussbaum's central human capabilities deal with the concept of a list that is absolute and demands compliance (Nussbaum, 1999; Feldman and Gellert, 2006). Cross-cultural norms used by Nussbaum discount people's freedom to live their lives in ways they want to. In her defence, Nussbaum (1999) stated that cross-cultural norms advocate political liberty and protect people's freedom and choice from value systems that work against universal norms of equality and liberty, such as women's rights. Nussbaum does not direct what should be done but holds countries accountable to universal norms of equality and liberty. Feldman and Gellert (2006) suggest that Nussbaum may address inequality between countries but does not consider historical structures of inequality within countries. Within hierarchies of class, gender, politics and society that generate and perpetuate inequality, an abused woman may be given training and education, but this does not deal with the societal cultural hierarchies that facilitated her abuse. Sen and Nussbaum's capability approach does not adequately deal with the sources of inequality in emphasising what a person can do and the life they ought to lead. Developing capability may enhance the individual's life but does not sufficiently address the (historical) conditions which the individual is still affected by or within which is still denied capability.

For low-income female teachers, what they view as a meaningful life may reproduce structural inequalities through social reproduction, but it does provide a local understanding of capabilities from their experiences as women and teachers within their local community. The idea of capabilities, freedom of choice and aspiration has impacted Indian education policy significantly, which in turn implemented policies destructive of the teacher's role and student progression. This is core to understanding teacher agency and values among those most vulnerable to marginalisation within the education system, the low-income female teacher.

Another main concern with the capability approach is the question of what constitutes a valuable functioning or a basic capability. Sen views commodities as leading to freedom but not the extent of freedom; people should be able to use goods to pursue diverse interests and objectives. Sen states this as 'actual freedom' where through action and doing, one exhibits a utilitarian mastery through one's capability (Crocker, 1992; Sen, 2005; Feldman and Gellert, 2006). In essence, actual freedom is the ability to use commodities to pursue individual interests as part of one's individual capabilities. This emphasis on a person's ability to choose and create a meaningful life for themselves places 'capability' as key to an individual's freedom of choice. Education as a commodity is used by the individual to enable them to lead a valuable life, through their individual action. Education, therefore, enables a student to have a life in which choice and individual capability are afforded to them. In contrast, research within India found that neoliberal emphasis on individual economic achievement through education impacted the duties of the teacher in the classroom and conflicted with individual and mutual family obligations for the student.

Influenced by the capability approach, teachers felt frustrated over government pressure to audit and improve academic achievement results by increased administrative duties to fill out multiple attendance and marks registers (Mooij, 2008; Triveni, 2014). Teachers' practice was reduced to facilitating external directives that led to teacher demotivation (Smail, 2013; Batra, 2014). Local government inspection of schools mainly involved inspecting paperwork without engaging in teaching observations, reducing the significance given to practical teaching practice (Mooij, 2008). Teacher frustration was deepened by a lack of compensation for additional duties. This is a common enough experience among teachers elsewhere, where a focus on academic achievement and use of standardised tests have contributed to a shift in how a teacher is viewed (Berliner, 2001; Hattie, 2003; Campbell et al, 2004). Within India, the conflict is underlined by the traditional and cultural significance attached to the role of the teacher within society. Teacher demotivation is reinforced by a loss of social standing and respect as their administrative duties increase and their teaching practice is undervalued (Mooij, 2008; Smail, 2013).

The impact of neoliberal policies on the lives of young people can be destructive for those unable to meet high standards of exam performance and having a choice towards a meaningful life. As part of the 'Young Lives Project' (Morrow, 2013), research within Andhra Pradesh found that pressures to pass secondary school exams were influenced by the need to access pre-university and higher education to secure future employment and financial stability. This led young people who did not pass their exams to develop a deep sense of failure and feel the loss of a better life. Morrow found that this sense of failure and loss was mediated by invoking fate as the ultimate marker of destiny. Young people used fate to balance their own aspirations with family responsibilities and duties. Students' strong obligation to family, through financial support or taking care of younger siblings, influences their individual aspirations achieved through coveted secondary school qualifications. Higher value placed on positions such as that of doctor compared to lower valued traditional vocations of agricultural work mark a shift in values for young people. Formal qualifications promise greater economic stability and ensure better marriage prospects and greater social mobility. The individual desires of students are intertwined with family relationships, social aspirations and personal companionship. Intergenerational mutuality and family relationships conflict with universal neoliberal policies focusing on individual development and aspiration (Morrow, 2013).

Despite a motivation to enable people to lead diverse and meaningful lives, considering local circumstances and environment, leading a meaningful life is not strictly about individual choice but involves mutual relationships. Sen has allowed for social interdependence but sees this as essentially meeting societal obligations; an individual is socially validated and accepted through their material possessions, skills or status acquired through education (Crocker, 1992; Anand and Sen, 2000). Meeting societal obligations preserves human dignity and maintains one's social standing but does not account for complex areas where obligation is mutual and reciprocal, between the individual and their family or community. Within social interdependence as defined by Sen, it is clear what is expected for an individual to meet social obligations. The individual is somewhat separate from that upon which they are dependent; they need to fulfil or meet those expectations to be accepted, and society needs them to do so to function as a society itself. Individuals in this context are given varying opportunities and agency to meet them.

The reciprocal nature of aspirations and values that determine social interdependence within India are complex because such values are not only shared by both the individual and the family or community, but are intertwined between them and are fluid. It is difficult for the individual to separate themselves from such obligations or define them as discrete values. The fluid nature of shared values and aspirations means that these move and flow between people, but not always within equal positions of authority or power. Despite values being shared and flowing between parent and child, teacher and student, it is often those in subordinate positions who are obligated to accept those values and aspirations.

Dignity and preserving individual freedom through individual aspirations conflict with the social and cultural contexts in which Indian teachers operate (Ramachandran, 2003). Mutual obligation between an individual and their collective context – whether it be society and family or between teacher and student – can help us understand the context in which female teachers negotiate their social relationships and define their agency. It can also help us understand the entangled nature of social relationships that reflective practice needs to consider when supporting female teachers within India. It is important to consider whether these have been integrated into recent initiatives to professionalise teacher training within the National Education Policy (NEP, 2020).

National Education Policy 2020 and revision of teacher education

The National Education Policy (NEP, 2020) outlines bold steps to professionalise teacher education by dissolving independent teacher training institutions and placing training within higher education. By 2030, an integrated four-year BEd (Bachelor of Education) will be the required qualification; this offers a dual degree of a bachelor's degree of two years within a subject specialism (BA/BSc) and two years of a BEd. Those who have a three-year undergraduate degree can still access the two-year BEd that has been traditionally offered

Figure 1.2: NEP 2020, length of study and options for prior degrees

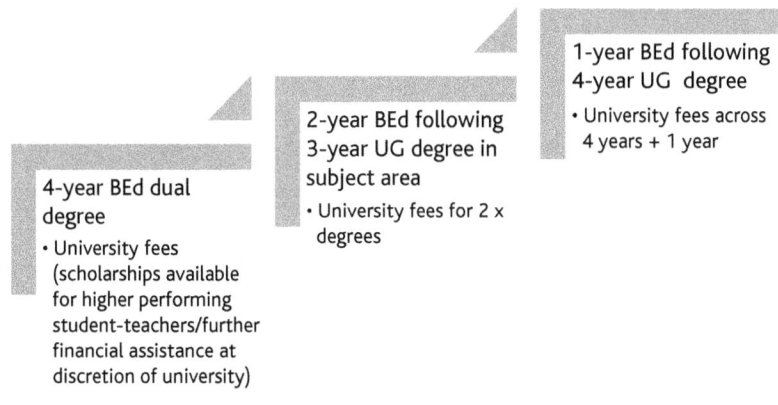

(see Figure 1.2). Aligned with this is a distinct move to professionalise teaching through continuing professional development for those wishing to use industry experience to teach and within universities. PhD students will be offered credit-bearing courses on pedagogy to facilitate future academic careers. The motivation behind moving teacher education to multidisciplinary higher education institutes is to have greater central control of teaching quality and avoid widespread corruption where training institutions provided inadequate and substandard training (Singh Dhillon and Bharti, no date; Alam and Debnath, 2022).

The basic requirement of a four-year integrated degree is to prepare teachers to obtain subject knowledge along with teacher training within multidisciplinary universities and under a specific department of education. While there are many positives to this – and certainly one of them is the move to stamp out corruption and improve quality within teacher training – placing teacher education within universities does not guarantee a higher quality of teachers nor does it improve access for a large demographic who train to become teachers, that is women who negotiate complex social and family obligations to train to teach and gain employment. This is exemplified in the financial costs and length of time studying that the four-year degree entails for women whose access to higher education is socially and culturally impeded. As will be seen in Chapter 2, teacher motivations to go into teaching are aligned to supporting their family and work, and teaching is a safe and acceptable option for them. These new changes brought about by the NEP 2020 can discourage those women who have chosen teaching as a means for financial stability with the higher financial costs and time needed for study.

In Bangalore, at the time of writing, only two higher education institutions currently offer the four-year degree. For one of them, the tuition fees and accommodation across the four years amount to INR 11,88,000 (£11,850), or INR 297,000 per year. Food costs are expected to be between INR 5,000–6,000 per month. To place these fees into context, according to the minimum wage rates for 2022 from the Karnataka State Labour Commission Office, an average middle income position as a junior doctor brings in INR 40,000 per month (INR 4,80,00 pa) with lab technicians and radiographers with a BSc receiving an average INR 12,944 per month (INR 1, 55,328 pa) (State Government of Karnataka, 2022a). There are variances between different employment positions and level of skill. Domestic employment, a category that includes mainly low-income women, brings in an average of INR 14,000 per month (INR 1,68,000) for central Bangalore (State Government of Karnataka, 2022b). In contrast, the average salary for a software engineer in the affluent IT industry within Bangalore is INR 83,333 per month (INR 1,000,000 pa) (Glassdoor, 2023).

Scholarships are offered for those whose family income is below INR 4 (£4,000 pa), with scaled percentages of scholarship for different income levels. For women who traditionally completed a two-year BEd either before or while teaching, the additional fees that come with a dual degree bring another barrier to higher education and employment. For lower-income women, the challenges are greater. Not only do they need to obtain teaching qualifications that require twice the time taken for study, and where they are not earning or contributing to their family income and responsibilities, but the scholarship assistance outlined by the NEP (2020) is dependent on candidates' outstanding academic achievements in secondary school and pre-university. It is notable that the university in Bangalore asking the cited fees for their four-year degree offers scholarships based on financial income and not on academic merit; this is a move that I hope other universities will follow.

Although it is commendable that scholarships are offered to those most capable, this does further displace those who were unable to meet the high standards of secondary school examinations within India and increases pressure on exam performance as a way to obtain future education and employment. Access to quality education within high school is not an absolute within India. Prospective student teachers are disabled from entering the profession at the school level itself, even more so if, as a girl, you have additional responsibilities within your household and face pressure to marry and look after your husband's family. If scholarships are based on academic merit, low-income groups must be afforded equal opportunity to achieve these through the quality of their school education provided by teachers who are suitably supported and trained.

The length of time studying for the four-year degree does favour those with the income and family context to support this. This is the minimum requirement. However, those holding a three-year undergraduate degree can undertake the two-year BEd traditionally offered, with a third option for those who have completed a four-year degree of a one-year BEd specifically adapted to teach a specific subject specialism. Those who have prior degrees are able to develop increased subject specialist knowledge to those taking the two-year minimum subject requirement for the four-year degree. This privileges those with the ability to pay for and obtain a higher level of specialist knowledge. This is in turn enables them to be able to teach at higher levels and command higher salaries. The two-year subject specialism affords less time to obtain subject knowledge to take to the classroom, thus decreasing the subject knowledge needed to teach and contributing to a lowered social status.

Two classes exist within these revisions, one that can either pay for the four-year degree or have academic merit to receive a scholarship and the other that has had the resources to gain prior three- and four-year degrees before choosing to teach. Those that cannot meet the financial and entry requirements of the new degree are further removed from a traditional source of income, especially low-income women for whom teaching was a route out of poverty for themselves and their families. Moving teacher education into higher education could result in greater pressures and barriers to those from low-income groups, especially women, to undertake a lengthy and costly degree. Teacher education within the NEP 2020 emphasises subject knowledge and academic achievement over the value of social relationships and non-academic support that teachers bring to the classroom. If teachers from low-income groups are discouraged from entering the profession, students within low-income schools will lack the local experience, connection and relationships that local teachers bring with them.

Options are available for teachers within Early Childhood Care and Education (ECCE) (NEP, 2020) who are traditionally female. Those with secondary and pre-university education can receive a six-month certificate programme and those with lower educational qualifications a one-year diploma programme in early literacy, numeracy and other areas of ECCE. This provision does support early learning, but it may be the main option for women with limited choice. Primary school teachers do not receive the same – higher – salary of secondary school teachers and, if this is the main option for women on a lower income, this further disallows access to a higher salary and training beyond a role that is traditionally seen as female-oriented and domestic.

Placing teacher training within higher education may help standardise the delivery of training, but it does not answer a central problem that affects most schools in India: the need for teachers to engage actively with their current teaching practice to improve their teaching and support student learning. Teacher training within a university environment does not necessarily guard against low quality teaching; it neither imbues the teaching profession with any higher status nor ensures that teachers can indeed support students in critical independent thinking. This is especially significant if teacher training continues to be maintained through central control and administration following its move to universities.

BEd programmes have been designed and disseminated through state and central government administration. By moving delivery from teacher training institutes to universities, the autonomy of higher education institutions is placed into question (Gupta, Gupta and Choubey, 2021). Moving a BEd programme from independent teacher training institutions to universities is not just a shift to a venue where there are tighter controls on corruption, it also introduces the teacher to a multidisciplinary university learning environment. As such, the BEd that accompanies a dual degree or is taught as a standalone requirement must adapt and evolve to modules that engage student teachers with higher level pedagogical content as well as enabling critical thinking in independent learners who, aside from theory, utilise learning experiences in their classroom practice.

The BEd syllabus put forward by the NCERT (National Council of Educational Research and Training, 2016) emphasises practice as part of the two-year programme. The final semester of 18 weeks, following an internship, focuses on inclusive education, gender and society, and the arts, including a generic unit on 'understanding the self'. This unit includes distinct reflective practice objectives, such as understanding oneself in relation to society and an abstract analysis of the self as individual within society. It is indeed commendable to include reflective practice within a BEd syllabus, especially as it introduces student teachers to creative means of expression. Student-teachers are encouraged to engage in narratives, poetry, humour, case studies and films where the subject has discovered their potential to develop a variety of reflective practice techniques.

There are, however, key areas where the principles of individual reflective practice conflict with the unit design. A way of dealing with conflict is included but emphasises social harmony by drawing on 'collective strengths' that use reflective practice to develop a humane professional persona (National Council of Educational Research and Training, 2016, p 130). By highlighting a collective sense of self and social harmony, the unit does not support future teachers to engage in critical or deeper engagement with a self that may be inherently contradictory or fragmented. Reflective practice and discovery of self is repurposed to subsume the individual within the collective, not necessarily to draw out a greater understanding of oneself and one's professional persona, which is crucial preparation for classroom practice. Understanding who you are as a teacher and what you can bring to the classroom as part of your unique contribution to students can help teachers identify strengths and areas for improvement.

In addition, the specific space of the teacher within Indian society is not covered. Student-teachers may develop technical reflective skills, but how do these support a practical application of such skills in one's immediate and everyday experiences within and outside the classroom? The student-teacher is trained in reflective practice techniques and interesting, creative methods to understand themselves. They are essentially equipped with skills that they have not fully practised or experienced. They are expected to develop efficacy in reflective practice skills without practising these within long-term teaching experience and the daily everyday nature of teaching.

Applying theory to practice is starting to emerge in programmes designed for the four-year BEd. A paper/module on the 'Psychology of learner, learning and instruction' from Ajmer University, (Ajmer University, no date, p 75) includes a unit on 'Learning through constructivism' that outlines theories as well as the role of the teacher and learner within constructivism. Especially exciting to see is a unit on creating a learning environment that includes implementing active learning. This all looks wonderful to read and is supported by an outline of assessments that enable imaginative contributions through written reflective assignments, field observation notes and case study analysis. However, a final written test is included as a final assessment for the paper. Within a unit that covers the benefits of active learning and underwritten by constructivism, assessments that prioritise written exam performance conflict with and further disable opportunities for learning beyond the scope of the BEd. Another example of a resource within a four-year programme includes a reflective diary during a 16-week school placement with instruction to maintain daily reflections and teaching (Department of Education, 2019). This is a step in the right direction by including reflection during the school day; however, there is limited or no mention of reflective practice theory or cycles that can support reflection. There seems to be a need to include these terms but minimal pedagogical support to embed reflective practice into school placements for use beyond their degree programme. Reflective practice is foundational to understanding your teaching practice and identifying areas to develop as a teacher. Continually assessing your impact on student learning is key to teaching that considers the challenges and environment in which teaching and learning occurs. Improved teaching skills within socially deprived areas impact the ability of students to achieve an education and contribute to securing their financial stability. Improved teaching can lead to social mobility and social transformation, with teachers at the forefront of effecting social change.

Reflective practice that supports teaching practice is crucially needed within teacher education in India and is not suitably outlined or addressed by the NEP 2020. BEd programmes that act as one half of a dual degree or are offered alone will continue to prepare student-teachers to be technically reflexive so as to fulfil assessment criteria, but not as an active preparation for their future teaching practice. This is exemplified in contradictory and conflicting programme design, where a summative learning model is often used to assess learning outcomes that are based on principles of continual learning. Dyer et al's (Dyer et al, 2002, 2004) attempts to develop reflective practice among Indian teachers found teachers had difficulty identifying problems within their teaching practice, but this is the initial stage within the reflective process.

Being unable to identify problems with your teaching can be attributed to a learning environment that places a moratorium on learning once a person is employed and in a position of authority. However, the disconnect between theory and practice and prevalence of summative learning is far more complex than Dyer et al allude to. Reflective practice within teacher education fundamentally discounts the teacher's lived experiences within and outside the classroom that extend beyond a daily record of teaching to how these experiences shape their teaching practice. It discounts these experiences because it views these teachers as passive recipients of pedagogy theory and teaching techniques, not active learners who can design, deliver and evaluate their teaching. This is very much at the heart of this book. The rote learning model that teachers employ within the classroom is a product of the way in which they have been taught at school and in teacher training programmes. It is part of a deep-rooted historical and cultural attitude to knowledge, position and authority.

The key Issues that prevent effective reflection practice within India go beyond a distinction between summative and continual learning. It is not sufficient to point to exam performance or how tests and quizzes are prioritised in the classroom as the reason why teachers find it difficult to identify problems in their teaching. Indeed, there has been much discussion around assessment change from exams to coursework to support Indian students. But this does oversimplify the situation and polarises the deeply complex set of barriers to achievement that an Indian student faces. These barriers within the education system in India, and within Indian society itself, limit the contribution of those most marginalised by social, economic and policy displacement towards effective reflective practice in India: namely, what those most forgotten and most undermined can tell us through their narratives and stories about ways to improve teaching quality through reflective practice within India. They are the recipient of policy and directives, but through their stories and experiences they can provide a counter voice to those designing and delivering BEd programmes that prioritise theory over practice.

Towards the lived experiences of low-income female teachers

It is the voice of the low-income female teacher that underlines the foundations of this book – in particular, the value of their perspectives and experiences in helping to support effective reflective practice within India. What can these teachers tell us about how they see their practice, how they negotiate their personal and professional lives? What does this tell us about how reflective practice can be further developed within teacher education to support a significant demographic of the teaching population to improve their teaching? In essence, how can the values and agency as expressed by the low-income female teacher support a revision of how we teach reflective practice to our teachers that may in turn support the evaluation of the teaching profession, and professional practice itself, within India?

Three main themes run throughout this book, focusing on how the values and agency of low-income female teachers can support reflective practice within teacher training programmes. These are:

- the significance of the low-income female teacher voice in how we understand achievement, aspiration and freedom of choice for our students and ourselves;
- insight into how low-income female teachers view their practice and negotiate their personal and professional lives;
- how understanding female teacher agency that supports their empowerment within the classroom can help our understanding of teacher effectiveness.

Issues of representation in examining shared values of teachers

The number of studies calling for greater cultural relevance in education research in India (Mooij, 2008; Joshi, 2009; Ganapathy-Coleman, 2014; Menon et al, 2014) contributes to understanding local environments and contexts through focused studies of target groups. However, this can be complicated when considering the issue of representation for marginalised groups and multi-layered contexts of Indian society and culture.

Culturally relevant research can be seen to mark out a distinct space in which research focuses on specific groups in response to a need to study the uniqueness of a group and the particularities of their culture (Spivak, 2005). Singular, focused research is beneficial in highlighting groups that have been disadvantaged by progressive agendas. A multitude of singular studies focusing on different groups is valuable when we examine the diverse and complex context of India but can be problematic when attempting to examine shared values among groups that span local regions and are grouped together by their profession, such as teachers. Each study that looks at specific cultural meanings of a specific group results in the differences between each group and study as the distinguishing characteristic of each group.

They are identified through their difference from each other within a multi-layered and multi-faceted society. This can pose problems for research that prioritises the individual within the group, such as the individual teacher within a group of teachers, but does not seek to impose overarching characteristics to understand them. How can research be conducted for a group defined by their lower-income status, gender and profession that does not result in another singular study whose difference and uniqueness disallows their relevance beyond the scope of their demographic and locality? The key issue for me here is how the dynamics of self-representation in terms of how these teachers choose to represent themselves can transcend the boundaries of their singular experiences so that their lived experiences have value beyond cultural relevance and towards representation.

The conditions in which the low-income female teacher is enabled to represent themselves through self-examination need to consider the impact of reflection and self-representation. The central concern with representation for these teachers lies with the inequalities in which they are embedded and which they experience implicitly. Self-reflection could bring about changes to their lives that may be at odds with the cultural and social contexts they are dependent on (Freire, 1996; Spivak, 2005; Robinson-Pant and Singal, 2013b). If inequalities that one has accepted and not questioned are brought to the surface, this could bring about disruption to these teachers' lives that they or their families and communities may not be prepared for.

Freire (Freire, 1996) outlines oppressors as those with power and authority over the oppressed, those who have been subjugated within oppressive structures. In their bid to emancipate the oppressed, former oppressors continue a form of oppression despite their good intentions. Their prejudices towards the oppressed's ability to think and act for their freedom surface in their inherent distrust of their capabilities. Hence, they act and think for them, disabling true emancipation. Oppressors recognise that change must happen, but that change must come from those in positions of authority, a top-down transformation. This is so far in accordance with issues of representation as outlined by Spivak (2005), but it is the act of reflection and Freire's emphasis on self-regulation that pose problems for encouraging reflection among subaltern teachers.

Freire asserts that those within positions of authority need to open themselves up to examine their motives and desires for their actions stating, 'those that authentically commit themselves to the people must re-examine themselves constantly' (Freire, 1996 p 42). Within education, the teacher occupies an asymmetrical positional authority and must examine their inherent distrust of their students' learning by examining their own prejudices and personal attitudes to their student cohort and to their teaching practice. Self-examination is defined as self-regulation in a clear moral motivation to improve oneself to affect change. Acknowledging power relations enables a closer engagement with authentic self-improvement and moral development. This requires a continual examination and relearning of one's personal values and how they emerge or manifest in professional interactions.

The need for self-reflection to engage with prejudices and attitudes to one's students may present problems for those whose attitudes and values are not only implicit and socially and culturally embedded but for whom the act of reflection can destabilise local circumstances, family and social obligations within which they are mutually dependent. The conditions in which self-examination occurs among low-income female teachers must consider complex areas that utilise cultural references and power relations within an entangled and intertwined space. A key concern is whether teachers can untangle and examine these spaces and the extent to which it can be done. Therefore, the issue of representation in relation to conditions in which self-reflection occurs ought to be determined by the teacher and not those in positions of power.

Research design and rationale

Fundamental to my research is that knowledge is derived from individual experiences and perspectives. Individuals can construct and define reality as understood and experienced by them. These understandings provide valuable insight into sections of society that are not part of a majority, specifically the lives of marginalised groups and minorities. Therefore, this research is guided in part by my understanding of knowledge and reality as constructed by the individual, the value of which lies in their ownership of their perspectives and experiences and its contribution to a wider understanding of social reality.

A constructionist ontological position defined teachers' individual interpretations as central to my research (King, Keohane and Verba, 1994; Cohen, Manion and Morrison, 2007). Concepts surrounding teacher values are products of individual understanding and meaning. These may be multiple, entangled and specific as well as delineated by how the individual teacher constructs such meaning (Guba and Lincoln, 1994).

I used a postpositivist framework that did not believe human behaviour is ruled by universal laws or causal behaviour (Guba and Lincoln, 1994; Creswell and Miller, 2000; Cohen, Manion and Morrison, 2007). An interpretivist approach helped design and collect data, where theory surrounding teacher values was to emerge from teacher responses, comprising diverse insights and meaning. The individual voice of the teacher highlighted how they navigate societal and cultural expectations. As already mentioned, the voice of the teacher is central and acknowledges the impact of social and cultural norms within individual perspectives.

Relying on causal relationships to link human behaviour and responses to historical and cultural tropes, such as a guru–shishya relationship (traditional teacher–student), places the contemporary teacher as a product of long-standing social, institutional and cultural practices (Cohen, Manion and Morrison, 2007). I did not intend to infer causal hypotheses in relation to the views of teachers. I did not want to look at what caused them to think the way they do but rather to understand how they describe their social context (King, Keohane and Verba, 1994). I did not want to generalise complex and individual meanings behind experiences into nomothetic social and cultural structures, as is common among education research within India. I wanted to avoid sublimating the teacher's voice into causal factors that would take priority over their words. The internal, private thoughts and feelings of teachers are their own and what may be expressed to myself may be a self-conscious act. I wanted to examine this self-conscious act itself, specifically the way teachers may construct their speech in dialogue with me as the primary object of study, focusing, therefore, not only on what teachers were saying but how they were saying it.

I have specifically sought out idiographic knowledge that is subjective, unique and particular to the lived experience of teachers. I believe it can open individual perspectives of a demographic who have often been subsumed into overarching and causal interpretations of their teaching practice. An idiographic approach can enable a richer understanding of how these teachers as individuals with unique histories and experience engage with their social world (Cohen, Manion and Morrison, 2007). We should also consider that, while individuals do not necessarily respond mechanistically to their environment, their views are not completely independent from their environment (Prosser and Trigwell, 1997; Cohen, Manion and Morrison, 2007).

Phenomenography offers a non-dualistic approach in understanding how teachers interpret certain events in their own and their students' lives, including the environment in which they operate (Prosser and Trigwell, 1997). The phenomenon is their teaching practice and views on the changing social, cultural and economic environment in India. Variation is a key element of phenomenographic research, where diverse meanings and views reveal different ways of experiencing a phenomenon. In my attempt to analyse different meanings, structural relationships between these meanings were created with internal hierarchies between different definitions and words used (Åkerlind, 2012; Tight, 2016). Termed as the 'output space', Åkerlind states, this can provide a collective, holistic view of different ways in which people experience the same phenomena. Phenomenographic research is particularly useful as it focuses on variation and commonalities of individuals within a sample group and not necessarily on the variation of meanings and opinions within an individual narrative. The individual teacher's responses are viewed in conjunction with how they relate to others being interviewed as a variation within a collective narrative.

Although the individual voice is prioritised within my research, I was concerned that the teacher may get incorporated into a larger set of collective data within my sample group when comparing variation and commonalities. I did not want to lose the individual voice while comparing it to other voices in the same group. Therefore, it was important that there were two levels of data collection: one in which the teacher explored attitudes and views on their own and one in which they explored such views within a group and as part of a collective. This research design made it possible to gain further insight into teacher attitudes when examined in these two different contexts. The teacher could narrate their life history with or without a structured form of questioning, make their own connections and attribute meaning through narration and reflection. In the group context, they could participate in discussion where their individual interpretations were examined on how they negotiated and engaged with the group. My research focus was not how the teachers operate as a group or collective, but how the individual teacher participated and negotiated their individual views within the group (see Figure 1.3).

My research was conducted in Bangalore, South India. Bangalore is a vast cosmopolitan city with distinct localities and separation between the north and south of the city, where I conducted my research,

Figure 1.3: Research design with individual and group interviews

- Individual (exploratory/history)
- Individual within the group (negotiation/relationships)

Individual and group interviews

- Narrative, idiographic knowledge
- Variation between individual views and within group context

Nature of individual views on their own and within a group

- Voice/own connections/own meaning
- Individual negotiation within the collective/group

Data analysis focus

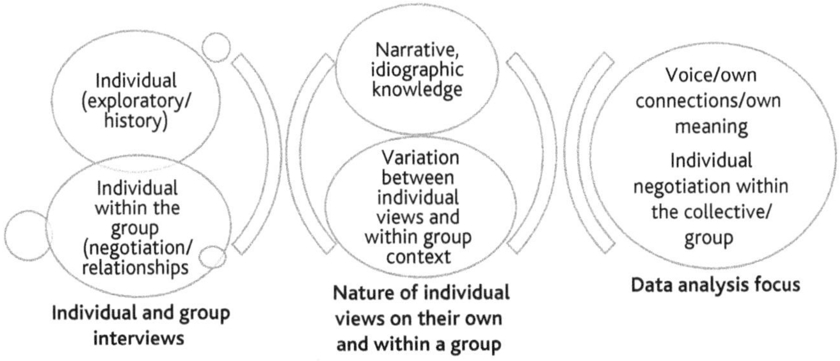

has traditionally been the cantonment area where British officers either retired or were stationed. Its colonial history is reflected in the design of streets, street names and colonial bungalows with porches or verandas. It is now a widely English-speaking part of the city with a significant international and expatriate community, including local Anglo-Indian communities. Schools are more widely sought after as they are high-performing, private English-medium institutions with a strong colonial history. South Bangalore has a strong local Kannadiga community with local Kannada medium schools, streets organised in blocks and a larger Hindu population.

Two English-medium high schools, School 1 and School 2 with low-income students, agreed to participate in my research in Lingarajapuram, North Bangalore. Female teachers from typically low social status backgrounds are often indicated by economic status and traditional caste status. These would be traditionally the farmer (Vaishya) and labourer (Shudra) castes, including those considered as the lowest caste, the Dalit caste. Although caste would have been a useful marker for teacher profile, distinctions made regarding caste during requests for interviews were not considered appropriate and may have been misconstrued by school management. Managements were initially cautious and hesitant to allow their teachers to take part in my interviews. Singling out teachers from lower castes may not have helped assuage suspicions on their part. At the time of collecting data, female teachers earned between INR 8–10,000 per month.

In total, eight teachers participated in interviews, lesson observations and group discussions (see Table 1.1). Two teachers from each school were interviewed individually and had one lesson observed. These were

Table 1.1: Overview of distribution across interviews, observations and group discussion

	Teachers interviewed and lesson observed	Teachers as part of group discussion	Teachers per school
School 1	Amu Bhargavi	Gayatri Roopa	Amu, Bhargavi, Gayatri and Roopa
School 2	Celina Deepa	Lakshmi Savitri	Celina, Deepa, Lakshmi and Savitri

Amu and Bhargavi from School 1 and Celina and Deepa from School 2. They then participated with two additional teachers as part of a group discussion.

From School 1, Amu was a high school teacher who taught science. She had taught for six years in her current school and had achieved an MSc. She did not have a BEd. Bhargavi, the second teacher interviewed from School 1, taught English within the middle school. She had four years of teaching experience, with one in her current school. She had a BA but no teacher training qualifications such as the BEd.

Celina from School 2 taught maths and science at high school with 23 years of teaching experience. She had spent two years teaching in her current school. She had obtained a BSc but no formal teaching qualifications. Deepa taught science in middle school with seven years of teaching experience in her current school. She has achieved a BSc and MSc but, like the others, no formal qualifications such as the BEd.

These eight teachers through four in-depth interviews provided the rich data and content for the next three chapters. Their stories, ways of expressing and framing their opinions and views are truly fascinating. I am immensely grateful for their willingness to share their stories with me and for their words to take centre stage in my research.

In the next chapter, I will outline what they perceived of their roles as teachers and within their personal lives and how their means of sentence construction prompted a new direction in my data analysis that looked at spoken syntax and discourse analysis.

2

Teachers' perceptions of their roles

Chapter 2 examines how teachers viewed their roles within their professional and personal lives (see Figure 2.1). Social relationships play an important role in this, where relationships are mediated between female teachers and communities, peers, and students. Teachers' understanding of choice and freedom will demonstrate the complexities involved in achieving aspirations for themselves and their students. Social and family obligations are a crucial theme within this chapter and underline teacher views on shared ownership of knowledge and achievement.

Across Chapters 2, 3 and 4, relevant underpinning methodology will be introduced at the beginning of each chapter to place into context teachers' responses and my analysis. Chapter 2 introduces discourse analysis, as this was most appropriate for examining teachers' ways of speaking and emphasised the significance of speech within data analysis. Discourse analysis will be discussed following key sections of teachers' perceptions of their role. These include their motivations, their understanding of their relationships with students, and their personal and professional aspirations, followed by the role gender plays in these aspirations. The final section looks at the implications for reflective practice in teacher education.

Discourse analysis

Given that the main interaction with teachers was through interviews in which opinions and situations were discussed, discourse analysis

Figure 2.1: Chapter 2 outline

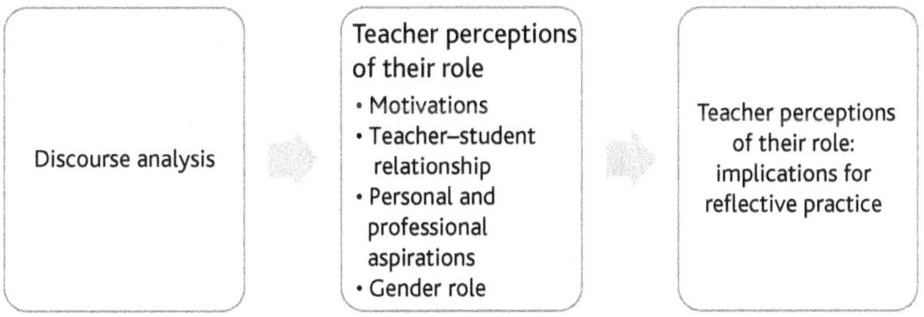

- Discourse analysis ⇒ Teacher perceptions of their role
  - Motivations
  - Teacher–student relationship
  - Personal and professional aspirations
  - Gender role
⇒ Teacher perceptions of their role: implications for reflective practice

was the most suitable method to conduct data analysis: it emphasises language as constructing meaning to express or describe one's ideas (Gee, 2005; Gee and Green, 1998; Willig, 2014). Discourse analysis helped explore the social language of teachers to uncover the context in which a vernacular emerges and delineates a group's identity. This includes teachers' underlying values and beliefs through the specific action of words they choose and how sentences and phrases are constructed (Gee, 2005). Linguistic construction revealed the social and experiential contexts which teachers constructed through the act of speaking and how they used language to do this (Willig, 2014).

Willig states that, although discourse analysis provides deeper understanding of how language can construct meaning and explicate social worlds, it does not explicate why certain words are chosen or discursive resources used. However, both Willig and Gee (Gee, 2011; Willig, 2014) state that discourse analysis does consider the context in which discussion takes place and looks beyond textual analysis to the participant's identity. Discourse analysis can, therefore, reveal how language develops into different styles and varieties to be associated with an identity. A key criticism of discourse analysis is privileging a distinctly social, institutional or psychological understanding of discourse rather than the thoughts and feelings of participants (Willig, 2014). As I was primarily concerned with the voice of the teacher, I focused analysis on ways teachers used language to infer meaning through their choice of words and descriptions. The individual teacher's thoughts and feelings specifically communicated to me were based on their choice of certain words and phrases and formed the basis of my analysis. I was interested in what they were trying to convey to me as an outsider rather than trying to seek out private or internal thoughts and feelings.

Although discourse analysis uses a variety of tools to analyse data, Gee (2011) does not advocate any order or rules of inquiry. However, Gee does state that an initial stage of discourse analysis can include analysis of grammar, syntax, writing and speech. This was a key stage of my data analysis.

The interviews were conducted in English, despite teachers' native language being Kannada, the regional language of Karnataka. A translator was not used as I did not want the interpretation of teachers' words to be filtered through a second person. When examining interview data, sentence construction and word order formed direct translations from Kannada to English but extended beyond basic transference from Kannada (subject–object–verb, SOV) to English (subject–verb–object, SVO).

Lange's (2012) research into Indian speakers of English revealed that spoken Indian English has produced a distinctive syntax in which Indian dialects reorder and interpret English syntax in four ways. The first two are topicalisation and left dislocation. Although not uncommon among British and US English, this is more common among Indian-English speakers. The topic is brought to the front of the sentence and becomes the main subject, moving subordinate clauses and the verb to the end of the sentence. This mirrors the subject–object–verb order of regional Indian dialects, including Kannada. For example, 'I will be going to school' (SVO) is restructured to 'I, school will be going'(SOV). The subject of the sentence is brought to the top, followed by the object being affected by the subject and the action or verb as a passive component at the end of the sentence. This sentence formation is quite significant to teacher responses discussed later in this chapter, especially in relation to active and passive teacher–student interaction. The third distinctive element in Indian English is using the word 'there' to indicate the existence of something that is non-specific and vague, such as the phrase 'Yes, it is there'. The fourth aspect is 'elliptical repetition', a way of being polite by repeating the other person's speech or phrases used. All four elements as outlined by Lange can be found within transcript extracts across Chapters 2, 3 and 4.

Linguistic research into Indian English has received some attention, whether to examine the structure of Kannada to English (Honnashetty, Reddy and Hanumanthappa, 2013) for computer programming or the technical development of bilingual speakers (Sridhar, 1992).

Most interesting is a study examining the 'Indianisation' of the English language (Kachru, 2016) with specific meanings that mainly English speakers within an Indian context would understand. Examples include words with a familial link, such as 'cousin-brother' or 'cousin-sister', or phrases, such as 'Do the needful'. Grammatical and phonological adaptations of the English language were a process of acculturation that was beyond simple transference from one language to another. The socio-cultural context was considered significant in defining an 'Indianism' as a distinct form of the English language that would not be wholly understood by an English speaker in another cultural context.

It is these forms of speech that will be examined in the rest of this chapter as teachers outline their views of their roles and social relationships.

Teacher motivations and aspirations within their personal and professional lives

Reasons to become a teacher

Amu and Celina's decision to take up teaching was prompted by their previous experience as a private tutor. It is common practice in India to have a private tutor who provides individual support that a schoolteacher with short lesson times and large class numbers cannot provide.

Researcher:	Why did you decide to become a teacher?
Amu:	This teaching profession first I was interested, then after certain days I joined this. Because from the beginning, I was interested … taking tuitions and teaching was my real interest. I love teaching.
Researcher:	What made you decide to go into teaching?
Celina:	Initially, I was taking tuitions, especially for orphans, (names local organisation) in the evening. They were generated from Mother Theresa, there I used to do the tuitions.

Amu and Celina's previous tutor experience introduced teaching founded in an individual relationship between teacher and student, where being a teacher is primarily based on the act of teaching and supporting the student. Celina clarified how her experience of tuitions helped with her teaching practice.

Researcher:	When you started teaching, what would you say is different between your first year and now?
Celina:	Because I had a practice of taking the tuitions and teaching them, that way was planted into the teaching level.
Researcher:	That gave you the experience?
Celina:	That gave me the experience.
Researcher:	How did you transfer teaching from tuitions where you were teaching one or two to a whole class?

Celina:	Tuitions is giving the individual attention to one person, but classrooms there is a further number of members, whatever we teach to one children [sic] it is equivalent to teaching the tenth child. We can't differentiate it. Then afterwards, I distinguished between the average, semi-average and the complete average.

One teaching context is transferred to another. Similar attention and dedication to the student is expected with no differentiation made between teaching a single student in tuitions or multiple students in a classroom ("whatever we teach to one children [sic], it is equivalent to teaching the tenth child"). The main difference is the student's ability in relation to the rest of the class, the student's 'average' ratio. Differentiation of abilities is related to a collective average ability. Despite giving individual attention, the student is still placed within a wider framework of performance characterised by average class performance. This reveals a discrepancy between stating that one gives individual attention to a student and classifying their abilities through an average or normative framework. The realities of the classroom inform how teachers adapt, despite statements saying they do not.

Amu provided further insight on why she loves to teach.

Researcher:	What do you like about teaching?
Amu:	Mainly like the children to get the knowledge and the other things are not throughout the life, but this knowledge what we give, it makes them to stand. We are the pillars so they can stand erect on that, so I love the best to do the children who are not doing it well.

For Amu, the teacher provides the student with ability to support themselves. The object of the teacher's focus is the student, placed above them as objects of their devotion and commitment ("it makes them to stand"), even if they are placed there because of knowledge passed onto them from the teacher as their pillar. The metaphor communicates the extent of their vocational commitment and values. The teacher as a pillar on which the students stand places the teacher as foundational support on which the student is erected and commands prime attention ("this knowledge what we give"). This could be an image of humility and modesty, of the teacher as hidden background support to their students' performance and achievement. The "pillar" referred to by Amu could be seen as a hidden support upon which students are elevated. However, this could also be a way of understanding the significance placed on the role of the teacher. They are the foundations on which students grow and develop; they are central to the learning process and classroom. The central role given to teachers by Amu revises the facilitator role introduced by child-centred policies. The teacher is not a guide but the foundation for student learning.

Teacher action is prioritised, with the student as a core objective of teaching, as outlined by Bhargavi and Deepa's descriptions of why they became teachers.

Bhargavi: [A]nyway, my education got over ... so that was the time I thought of this teaching profession ... so that was a very less salary ... beginning when I joined, I was paid below INR 1,000, only ... so with that salary, somehow I was working ... no other way ... then I thought of going again to the same office and working ... that was not working good for me ... so I felt let me do something to help children, those who don't know something ... teach them something ... an idea, a thought came to mind and that was that time I changed my profession.

Researcher: Why did you decide to become a teacher?

Deepa: Because lecturing, I feel ... they will do the lecturing and they will go ... no relationship between the student and lecturers ... as like one stranger they will come and they will go but teacher and students means they will bring the children ... they will look at like as a mummy or daddy ... because of half of the life they spend with us so whatever we say, this is the right way to bring up in their life but in their lecturing means after 17, 18 years they are grown up ... one proverb is there: 'as a small child we can bend but when they grow up we cannot bend'.

Bhargavi's decision to become a teacher was based partly on not wanting to work in an office environment but, as with Amu, teaching is equated with providing support to students who lack knowledge. What is significant is providing individual attention and knowledge to those who lack it ("those who don't know something"), placing the teacher as someone who has something to provide, to give. The act of teaching is therefore grounded in the act of giving, of providing and fulfilling a need as perceived by themselves. The relevance and need for the teacher are based on the notion that that they have something to impart to the student. Their value commodity is placed on their act of provision. This is supported by Kumar's (Kumar, 2010, 2011) outline of the subordinate provision role of women in India carrying on gendered expectations of care.

The teacher is an external force that pushes the student towards learning. Deepa prefers being a schoolteacher as opposed to a college lecturer. The schoolteacher acts as a parent to the student, providing maternal support during the day. Learning extends beyond classroom duties to supporting values, termed here as "the right way to bring up". The teacher as mother builds on the teacher as provider, where the motivation to teach for Deepa is to provide support that extends beyond classroom education and defined by a maternal care in teaching values to her students ("they will look at like as a mummy or daddy"). Teaching extends one's maternal role, one in which personal and professional lives coincide.

Deepa's metaphor of the student as malleable ("as a small child we can bend") is crucial to understanding how teachers approach their role as educators. They are providers with a strong influence on the lives of their students. The teacher is prioritised in this initial introduction to the teacher–student relationship within our dialogue. All four descriptions of why they became teachers were grounded in their ability to do something, to act upon a need, to fulfil their need to provide. While their professed focus is the student and their development, their initial understanding of their role as a teacher is to prioritise their own action. Although the student is central to their motivation, it is their own action and ability to provide education and values that is predominant ("this is the right way to bring up in their life").

The teacher's act of giving determines what is given by the individual teacher. Their knowledge is not just for individual consumption but to the wider community, as a form of communal sharing of knowledge and values underpinned by a sense of moral purpose.

The moral purpose of education and the role of the teacher

Shifts from doctrinal teaching from a religious frame to secular values of rationality and universalism mark a change in the role and purpose of education within society and, subsequently, in the role of the teacher. Ideals surrounding the purpose of education to serve the good of society have their foundations with Confucius, Aristotle, Aquinas and More who emphasised education as a form of 'moral enterprise', a means to ensure moral conduct and rules. Dewey and Durkheim sought to displace education's authority from religious morality (Dill, 2007). Durkheim (1963 as cited in Dill, 2007) felt religion needed to be removed from the classroom due to its perceived irrational tendencies and divisive nature, whereas Dewey promoted scientific inquiry as key to developing intelligence within the classroom, where values and morality are discussed and learnt (Dewey, 2011). The motivation was to develop minds that inquire rather than for students to just be disciples accepting the teacher's authoritative knowledge.

External sources of knowledge, such as religious sources, were seen to problematise value education. In support, Lovat (Lovat, 2013) references Habermas's notion of social engagement through praxis to disassociate a religious and moral doctrine from an education of values. The process by which authentic knowledge is developed and compelled through praxis to social action places education's role beyond that of a religious or moral frame into one of social justice. What is right or wrong, good or bad, is within a wider (secular) discussion of emancipation and liberty, of rights and inequality. Here, education's contribution to societal good shifts from religious-moral to secular-moral. Dill argues the use of values and negation of beliefs ignores strong motivations that some might hold sacred. Referring to one's 'beliefs' can reference secular and religious morals and is therefore more suited to contemporary culturally plural societies (Dill, 2007). A discussion of values within societies such as India, which have been traditionally culturally plural, necessitates closer examination of the interrelationship between religious, secular or cultural beliefs and values. Teachers' responses to why they decided to join the profession, despite the immediate need to contribute financially or be involved in an acceptable profession as a married woman, are framed as born out of the shared values and moral purpose that have been set by their families and which being a teacher enables them to enact. It is crucial to not discount this purposeful framing by Amu, Bhargavi, Deepa and Celina. It is important that they are not seen as just doing a job but that teaching has a specific higher purpose which is value-laden and moral in its performance.

Dewey, Durkheim, and Kohlberg's views of education can be seen to challenge the Indian teachers' moral role by introducing the teacher as primarily facilitating student experiential learning and cognitive development as a marker of teacher success and effectiveness. Dewey and Durkheim viewed education as a holistic development of the individual for the betterment of society, with Kohlberg viewing individual growth and cognitive development as achieved through one's moral development (Dill, 2007; Lovat, 2011). Kohlberg is critiqued (Lovat, 2011) as focusing education's role on cognitive skills. Cognitive development as a basis for achievement has underlined how school and teacher effectiveness are measured and underpins teachers' approaches to pedagogy (Klaassen, 2002; Campbell et al, 2004; Thornberg, 2008). Teachers both in the West and in India, indeed in Asia in general, are measured by the performance of their students. However, as noted in the teacher responses above, students within India are expected to contribute to their own achievement by following their teacher's instructions (Vijaysimha, 2013).

Defining the 'teacher and student' relationship

When describing their teaching style, the teachers prioritised themselves through their sentence structure. Teachers tended to frontload their action to the top of sentences or stanzas ('left dislocation') and leave student action towards the end of sentences and stanzas ('right dislocation'). Amu's description of her teaching style is a good example of this. In the extract below, left dislocation (LD) and right dislocation (RD) have been inserted to demonstrate how teacher action precedes student action in syntax.

Amu: So that is very important when we are teaching. Just I am teaching [LD] ... they are doing some work [RD] ... that will not work out. So first and foremost I stand up over there [LD] so everybody

> I can look there, each and every child's eyes should be towards us [RD] ... so what explanation we are giving or any example or any small thing or whatever we want, the classwork, checking or anything ... I stand up, I stand and I concentrate on that [LD] ... I see that each and every child will do the work what we say to them [RD].

The teacher's action is placed at the beginning of sentences while student action follows. One is active while the other is passive. Teaching is equated with classroom control, in which the teacher directs student action ("So first and foremost I stand up over there [LD] so everybody I can look there, each and every child's eyes should be towards us [RD]"). The students' eyes are to be fixed upon her, providing her with their full attention. The foundations of the teacher–student relationship are based on each enacting a role within the classroom. Bhargavi's description further illustrates the nature of teacher and student roles in the classroom.

Bhargavi: [F]irst time when I enter a class, whatever it is, I have the habit of saying some positive things to the children [LD] ... ok ... what are the good things they have to keep up ... cultivate in their mind so that will be helpful for them [RD] so once I finish the chapters ... I ask them [LD] 'Are you able to understand my explanation ... or I'm very fast or you cannot understand at all?' ... so I tell them [RD] ... I give them full freeness [sic] [LD] ... 'You can answer anything freely but I'll not scold you ... whatever is there, you just tell me' so that I'll change the method of teaching for you ... I'll tell the students, they are very friendly always and they'll cooperate in such cases so they'll say 'No miss, it is very nice' ... they can understand 'It is very interesting' they are saying [RD] ... once they answer, then I too understand that they understood the explanation what I have given.

Bhargavi's teacher action uses questions to students as recalled speech placed at the front and end of sentences as a way of illustrating her

Figure 2.2: Social relationship between teacher and student mediated by performance

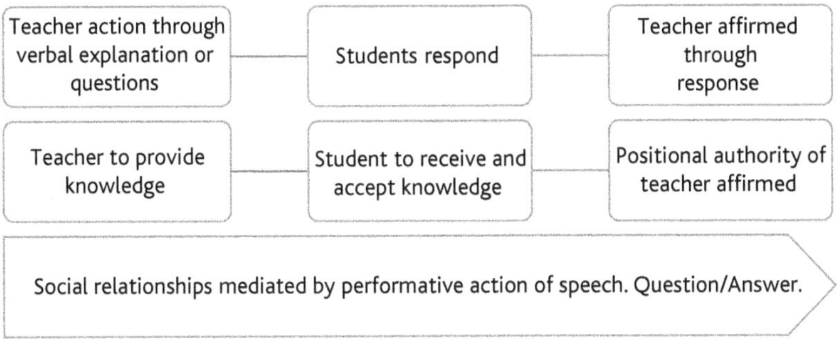

| Teacher action through verbal explanation or questions | — | Students respond | — | Teacher affirmed through response |
| Teacher to provide knowledge | — | Student to receive and accept knowledge | — | Positional authority of teacher affirmed |

Social relationships mediated by performative action of speech. Question/Answer. →

main teaching resource, her voice. The dominance of recalled speech reveals Bhargavi's teaching style as defined by performative action, of following a script within the classroom ("I give them full freeness [sic] [LD] … 'You can answer anything freely but I'll not scold you … whatever is there, you just tell me' … they are very friendly always and they'll cooperate in such cases so they'll say 'No miss, it is very nice' … they can understand 'It is very interesting' they are saying [RD]").

The teacher explains the text or lesson content and asks if students understand her explanation, students respond that they do and learning objectives are met, with the teacher's performance and skill validated and confirmed by student response (see Figure 2.2). If the role of the teacher is to provide knowledge, the role of the student is to receive and accept the teacher's explanations and positional authority within the classroom. Performative action is enacted in the classroom in which teacher and student follow a script and engage in verbal ritual and dialogue. Social relationships are defined by who speaks, who responds and in what form. This may be informed by historical caste and structural hierarchies in which social relationships are mediated by speech (Prickett, 2007; Joshi, 2009). The need to remain mute, to stay silent in response to discipline, to not speak or protest in response to outrage or to scold or admonish based on authority and hierarchy are parts of the social ties and mechanisms in which the teacher and student are embedded.

Despite Bhargavi stating she encourages students to be open about not understanding the lesson, her explanation of textbook material is what students must understand and therefore her skill in verbal communication and interaction with them is affirmed ("once they answer, then I too understand that they understood the explanation what I have given"). Students are left with little choice but to affirm their teacher's verbal explanations and maintain strong social ties and relationships within the classroom. It is best to nod or respond affirmatively as part of a wider set of social obligations that affirm positional authority within society in general, and certainly within the classroom.

The performative aspect of the teacher–student relationship was observed in lesson observations conducted by me. In Bhargavi's English lesson for Standard 7, mixed gender students sat in rows within the classroom. Classroom resources were a blackboard and chalk, with each student using a textbook and a notebook to write in. Bhargavi directed the lesson from the front, reading out a short story from the textbook while students followed along in their textbooks. Students were asked if they understood Bhargavi's explanations of key words and the meaning of the story, to which students responded verbally 'Yes, Miss' together as a group. Student contribution was limited to either group response to agree with the teacher or individual answers recalling the text and teacher's explanation.

Teachers' descriptions of maintaining order during classroom disruption can help us understand the importance of teacher and student performing and enacting their expected roles. Amu and Celina's descriptions of strategies used to bring students in line depend on their ability to control and direct students' attention.

Researcher:	But what about the students in your class, what goes through your head when they are misbehaving?
Amu:	I feel that he is not studying, or she is not studying … I want her to do whatever I am [LD] … the work we have given, they have to complete it [RD] … we have only this 40 minutes of time, so in that we have to do so many things [LD], complete our portions, they have to pay attention [RD] … first and foremost, what we explain … after listening also, so many children they won't be able to recollect it … then the learning outcomes must be there … outcome won't be there means what is the use of we giving so many explanations … so we need that … complete control should be there first [LD]. After the control, they will reason [RD]. Then after they take down, they will understand, they read that and come back, then only I get the learning outcome.

As seen in this extract, the teacher and student follow a strict process in which teachers disseminate information and students respond by taking it down. Amu fulfils the learning outcome when the students write down her explanations which demonstrates they have understood the teacher's explanation ("Then after they take down, they will understand, they read that and come back, then only I get the learning outcome"). Performing your role as a teacher or a student is crucial for the teacher to understand how effective her lesson has been, in particular her ability to disseminate information and control the classroom.

Celina demonstrates a more active role in disseminating information by focusing on the last bench, a position often reserved for lower performing students.

Researcher: How do you manage to reach the student in the last bench?

Celina: By asking them questions, directly I ask them. Sometimes, what happens, for example, notes is there, notes. The child is a very naughtiest child in the class, if you feel. If you can make that small child to come to the board and write. Actively it is given to that person to engage in some work, making him to engage in some work. I am doing something with the other students, so this person is distracting, so the distracting person should be brought to the concentration of the class. In that case, I make them to write the points on the board, what I tell.

As with Bhargavi, questions allow Celina to check student learning. The disruptive student can threaten the control and performance of the teacher, therefore by removing them from their physical space and into her's, she controls such disruption by creating disruption itself. She brings them from their usual space at the back of the class to the front as a form of disruption controlled by her. The teacher's performance to correct and maintain discipline while the student submits and eventually benefits is outlined by Celina ("so the distracting person should be brought to the concentration of the class. In that case, I make them to write the points on the board, what I tell").

The performance of expected roles and actions within the classroom demonstrate the continual re-enactment of positional authority held by the teacher in the classroom. It is through this performance of each other's roles that learning is seen to occur, whether this is through observing student behaviour through eye contact or verbally confirming understanding from a group response. It is vital for teachers to maintain the performative aspect of the relationship with students to assure themselves that learning occurs.

The deontic dimension of teaching is therefore underlined by the functional act of teaching, of acting as knowledge provider and ensuring learning through a performative relationship. By prioritising teacher action in their sentences, my interviewees can explain their sense of duty to their student as central actors in student learning and development of values. Teachers' sense of agency is predominant and influences their understanding of their role as educators. Within the teacher–student relationship, through the performance of their role in the classroom, they see themselves as enacting change and enabling student learning. This is significant to understanding how the teacher has perceived dominance in their students' lives as underlined by duty.

Character education ideal

In Dill's (Dill, 2007) comparison of Dewey and Durkheim, both viewed the classroom as a microcosm of society, in which learning rules can help instil a sense of duty and normative values through discipline. This is echoed in caring professions, including teaching. Carr (Carr, 2006), outlines the specific ethical and moral dimensions that govern occupations such as doctor and teacher as opposed to the ethics of occupations such as car mechanic. Both sets of occupations follow standard procedures and guidelines to fulfil the needs of those that depend upon them. However, Carr paraphrases Aristotle distinguishing between 'techne' and 'phronesis' to consider its ethical dimensions. Techne is concerned with the most effective means of doing something and phronesis considers the moral worth of such achievement. Carr suggests we may expect a mechanic to follow professional standards to repair our car but may also expect to be overcharged as we could be uncertain of their professional ethics that govern payment. We expect a doctor to treat us, but we also expect their treatment is conducted ethically as defined by their Hippocratic Oath. Carr's example outlines that the doctor and mechanic are positioned very differently in the service they provide when both provide similar services in diagnosis and treatment.

Carr distinguishes between a personal moral code of the mechanic to provide a reasonable quote and the professional ethics of being an advocate for another, whether it be one's health or education. The ideal phronesis of a teacher is their role as advocate with professional commitment to the overall development of the student as an individual and member of society (Hattie, 2003; Noddings, 2003; Carr, 2005; Brady, 2011; Lovat, 2011). The development of character within a student requires a certain type of person to teach them (Carr, 2005, 2006). This includes personal virtues that cannot be set or taught through standardised rules and regulations. The character education ideal demands that teachers possess and exhibit the values they teach and expect of their students.

A central criticism of character education is that it is essentially functionalist, serving an instrumental purpose and does not account for individual construction of values and identity within a poststructuralist domain (Campbell et al, 2004).

Values are based on beliefs that define an individual's attitudes and perspectives. These may be shaped by normative, societal values that incorporate moral and religious beliefs, including an individual construction of values. Values are also impacted by social, political and economic factors that contribute to understanding roles within society and individuals' contribution to it. A functionalist paradigm of education may not account for an individual construction of value within collective cultures such as India, where context and environment may impact an individual's construction of values. Context and environment are key here to understanding how teachers developed aspirations in conjunction with individual and shared values of their family.

Emancipation and freedom of choice

A crucial aspect when discussing teacher values in India is the relationship between emancipation and liberty, between 'freedom from' and 'freedom to' as approached by Western and Indian research studies. It is important to examine what is meant by emancipation and liberty of choice as it may offer different perspectives.

Giddens (Giddens, 1991) positions liberty of choice as developed from emancipatory politics that maintains a concern for freedom from traditional constraints and restrictions: 'Life politics does not primarily concern the conditions which liberate us to make choices: it is a politics of choice. While emancipatory politics is a politics of life chances, life politics is a politics of lifestyle' (Giddens, 1991, p 214). Giddens points to the self within life politics, as guided by a 'morality of authenticity' in its quest to be true to oneself through continual self-discovery. The self is empowered through a form of authentic living, where authenticity encourages the individual to construct oneself from restrictive structures. Social transformation within life politics allows one to rediscover oneself, including one's values. Life politics, in particular its emphasis on maintaining a set of values that do not perpetuate restrictive contexts, underlies research studies examining teacher reluctance and hesitation to enact a moral educator role (Klaassen, 2002; Thornberg, 2008).

Within Western research studies examining moral education (Klaassen, 2002; Thornberg, 2008), a central motivation surrounding teacher reluctance to engage in moral dialogue centred upon the individual choice made by the teacher to protect freedom of choice for their students. In addition, a lack of pedagogical knowledge was found in Klaassen's (2002) and Thornberg's (2008) studies examining such knowledge in teachers in the Netherlands and Sweden. Teachers recognised the importance of moral tasks and saw values education as instructional, focusing on 'how to behave' as the extent of discussion with students. Teachers had difficulty with carrying out their moral education role, ranging from a lack of professional knowledge and skills to support student dialogue on morality to a personal reluctance to engage with the moral domain for fear of putting forward authoritative values.

Teachers in these studies separated personal beliefs and values from their professional, instructional duties, exercising their freedom to choose and make decisions regarding their role and responsibilities as a teacher. Although these studies are not strictly concerned with emancipation and freedom, teachers' reluctance to engage in moral discussion indicates a tension between the teacher employing freedom of choice through adhering to an authentic dislike of authoritative frames, and the need to help students engage in a discussion of normative values. The issue lies in the teacher's freedom of choice to *not* engage in a discussion of values but perform an underlying emancipatory role preparing students to be valuable members of society. In contrast, studies examining the Indian teacher–student relationship indicate a strong emancipatory role, where the teacher and student are bound in a mutual duty to each other to improve the students' chance of being able to achieve the capabilities necessary to afford life politics, the freedom to make choices and decisions beneficial to themselves and their families. Mutuality of purpose between teacher and student are founded in the social realities outside the classroom and are best understood by examining how teachers described the personal and professional contexts which helped develop their aspirations.

Negotiating personal and professional contexts in developing aspirations

Negotiating personal contexts in teacher aspirations

Out of the four teachers interviewed, three provided details of their education and personal backgrounds in which their aspirations were first formed. Bhargavi and Deepa pointed to parents who made decisions about their future. Deepa initially had difficulty with her father making decisions for her, not with his role but in her inability to meet his expectations.

Deepa: [A]fter that I wanted to take commerce, to become like one officer, any official, like accountancy like that … I felt … but my daddy said 'No, not at all' … because he's a military man, so whatever he says, that you should do … he won't leave anyone, very strict he was but he was in military after that he got opportunity in postal service, he was post master, now he is retired. So, he put me in Science, there also I felt very difficult, I used to fail, in my life I never failed, I did not know failing marks. I told 'No, I can't' and even though lecturer used to go, 'If it is very difficult, after one month you can go to commerce, you can come', they used to tell you, that went in my mind, 'OK … I can come to commerce' so my daddy told, 'If you fail, ok no problem, once if you fail, second time you can fail, but third time you can do' … but now I am really very happy with my daddy what he had to say … because science has more opportunity in this world.

For Deepa, the negotiation took place between the expectations of her father and her need to follow his advice. She needed to adjust to her father's expectations as part of an internal struggle, one in which her fear of failure was to be resisted and overcome ("so my daddy told, 'If you fail, ok no problem, once if you fail, second time you can fail, but third time you can do' ... but now I am really very happy with my daddy what he had to say ... because science has more opportunity in this world").

What is not apparent is a conscious act of negotiation between an individual, preformed aspiration, and family obligations: not between an individual and a collective but the individual as part of the collective. Deepa correlates with Morrow's (Morrow, 2013) research into the interlinking of individual desires of students in Andhra Pradesh with those of their family. Morrow sees the issue as a conflict between intergenerational mutuality, family relationships and a neoliberal policy of individual development and aspiration. However, this conflict is not articulated within teachers' descriptions of their relationships with their parents. The conflict that is described is not between a collective society and an ill-fitting individualistic policy, but within the teacher needing to work on themselves to meet expectations. It is one of internal conflict in which one looks inward rather than outward between themselves and another ("I used to fail, in my life I never failed, I did not know failing marks. I told 'No, I can't'"). Negotiation is implicit and neither explicit in its action nor in the descriptions by teachers. It is part of the accepted role parents play in their children's lives.

In Bhargavi's case, her father and mother are part of normative family values supported through the distinctive roles played by father and mother.

Bhargavi: I want to say you know, my father doesn't like anybody to sit idle ... it's a daughter or a son ... he was working in the ITC [India Tobacco Company] ... he used to say 'When you are going to know about the house problems and all, not now then when you will come to know about these things?' [LD] ... So ... that things made us normal ... if we are coming across any problems ... now you are able to stand by the problem [RD] ... whatever it is in my life, I am ready to face the problem [LD] ... I have across such experience [RD] ... my father has brought up in such an environment, everybody is very supportive [LD] ... my mother is friendly with us ... but my father was a very strict person [RD] ... each and

> everything he used to take control of us [LD] ... so it was due to this pressure, now I am able to overcome all difficulties problems in our life [RD] ... because the support, that thing what he has taught us, now we have learnt that [LD] ... now I think of that ... what he did for us in the past, now we are able to stand by whatever problems come [RD].

In comparison to her mother's passive role, Bhargavi describes her father as active in instilling values that helped her to be resilient ("So ... that things made us normal ... if we are coming across any problems ... now you are able to stand by the problem [RD]"). As with Deepa, the father within the family is the main provider of learning, advice and direction, including being immovable and unrelenting in their instruction. Explicit negotiation – in which there is an actual exchange of intentions or desires to find a consensus or agreement – is not made apparent. It is more of an acceptance of systems in which one exists and functions that brings about long-term benefits ("but my father was a very strict person [RD] ... each and everything he used to take control of us [LD] ... so it was due to this pressure, now I am able to overcome all difficulties problems in our life [RD]").

Celina's description of her route into teaching reveals the impact of changing family circumstance on her personal aspirations.

Celina: We had a financial problem. Daddy was working. All of a sudden, his wages were changed [LD] ... I was 19 years old and I was doing my BSc second year, so because of financial problems [RD] ... the church did not provide us any help, we asked the church [LD] ... so I discontinued my BSc and I started working [RD]. Then I did my BSc by correspondence, mathematics.

Celina does not necessarily provide further explanation for why she needed to start working due to the loss of her father's job but the right dislocated statement "so I discontinued my BSc, and I started working" can serve as either a sufficient explanation or a passive statement within a framework of accepted systems and relationships where, if a parent loses their job, the child is expected to provide for their family. Celina does further qualify what led her to teaching:

Celina: So overall, I can say poverty pushed me into the teaching life, I did not get an opportunity anywhere. So I pushed myself, I went to (names school) that was my first job. At that time, I had discontinued my BSc.

Celina offers an alternative to the positive impact of parental influence during their children's lives. There is a distinct sense of being pushed into teaching as alternatives were not available. Circumstances which required her passive acceptance galvanised her into succeeding, despite having to give up her studies. Despite Celina pointing to poverty as a cause for her change in circumstances, the social structure in which she gave up her education to work is not alluded to or defined in any way. As with Feldman and Gellert (Feldman and Gellert, 2006), the underlying dynamics of social relationships and family obligations that perpetuate inequality are not made distinct.

Studying a different subject or discontinuing one's education to work is described through passive, matter of fact speech. There is a distinction between teachers' descriptions of their active role within the classroom and their passive role within their family. Bhargavi, Celina and Deepa place their action at the end of sentences, as passive actions in response to a parental action or cause. In doing so, they reinforce the asymmetrical relationship between parent/child, teacher/student in descriptions of their own family background.

In relation to their role as teachers, there does not appear to be a clear distinction between the normative values that teachers possess and those expected of their students. They are not outlined or explicated but accepted and implicit. Central to this are the implicit constructs and systems within which teacher and student, parent and child are embedded.

Negotiating professional contexts in teacher aspirations

Teachers' acceptance of asymmetrical relationships between parent and child, teacher and student define the professional context they work within. Key to this are shared aspirations between themselves and their students.

Amu outlines student learning as acquiring knowledge: her role is to instigate this:

Amu: Even the small class I enter, I pick up those kind of children and somehow I see that they have to do [LD], they should get the learning, they have to learn that knowledge, that wisdom ... each and everybody should have [RD].

The act of learning is to receive knowledge. Amu frontloads her action through her physical presence in entering the classroom and improving students learning ("pick up"), so that they become active in their acceptance of her instruction and in the act of learning. The idea that a student's learning is based on a foundation of teacher action is prevalent in teacher descriptions of their students.

Deepa: That is according to the lesson, some lessons no need to explain, already I have explained in the previous classes ... just I can say and go ... the meanings ... they will learn. But some lessons, they don't know, that I have to explain more.

Bhargavi: Utilising the children for learning different kind of things ... that is they will be learn outside, after they go home or maybe the parents cannot provide such things for the children, so I want whatever knowledge I have ... so for maximum, I want something to share with the students.

Celina: Devotion to studies. That should be there, devotion when he is devote-fully [sic] studying something, daily God will bless. One more thing, when he is doing on this path, he will be criticised. Criticision [sic] is a plus point for having knowledge. Somebody criticises you saying I don't know this, next day you'll come up with that.

Researcher: So when someone tells you, you don't know this, it is motivating for them?

Celina: Motivating.

Researcher: What is their relationship with their teacher? How should they be with their teacher?

Celina: With the same devotion.

Like Amu, Deepa and Bhargavi point to the teacher as introducing learning with their explanations and sharing knowledge ("just I can say and go ... the meanings ... they will learn" [Deepa]; "so for maximum, I want something to share with the students" [Bhargavi]), whereas Celina sees learning as devotion to their studies and to the teacher ("devotion when he is devote-fully [sic] studying something, daily God will bless"). This is also an area in which religious beliefs intersect with cultural values of gratitude to one's family and to God, and where devotion to one's learning is acknowledged and returned by God's blessing. As well as the teacher being a focal point in the act of learning, the student is viewed as deficient or lacking without the teacher instigating learning. This relates to literature on teacher identity in India (Sarangapani, 2003; Mooij, 2008; Sriprakash, 2011; Vijaysimha, 2013; Ganapathy-Coleman, 2014), in which the child is a symbol of inexperience, therefore needing adult guidance and direction to ensure their future success and achievement.

Bhargavi and Deepa's descriptions of parental influence on forming their aspirations correlates with the notion of the student not being fully aware of the world to make the right decision. The 'right decision' ensures future achievement as the consequences of making a wrong decision are more drastic within a context that lacks a stable and consistent welfare or benefit system. The child as an empty vessel needing to be filled with knowledge relates to the dominance of the guru ideal in which the student is shaped through instruction. Teachers' views of students are related to the emancipatory basis of the traditional guru, in which the student is saved through learning ("they should get the learning, they have to learn that knowledge, that wisdom ... each and everybody should have" [Amu]).

Student knowledge is built upon through teaching to prepare them for maturity and future achievement. This is a form of emancipation, of saving the student by ensuring future success, but it can also show the need to maintain social relationships between parent/child, teacher/student, in which emancipation is to be received from those in authority and at the top end of an asymmetrical relationship. Freire's ideas of emancipation put forward that those who are oppressed must represent themselves as a form of true emancipation (Freire, 1996). In this case, the act of saving the child, the student, requires both the active role of the parent/teacher and the passive acceptance of the child/student. The act of saving, of emancipation, is tied in with the act of learning and teaching. The way a child learns frames how aspirations are formed and in which a sense of achievement is perceived. It is shared between parent/teacher/child/student.

The culturally embedded ascetic ideal in the role of the guru

The historical role of the teacher as 'guru' is invariably discussed within Indian studies examining the socio-cultural context of the teacher. These include research on teacher demotivation (Mooij, 2008; Smail, 2013), policy efficacy (Sriprakash, 2011), teacher–student relationships (Gupta, 2003; Joshi, 2009; Smail, 2013; Ganapathy-Coleman, 2014) and use of teaching aids (Menon et al, 2014; Vijaysimha, 2013).

The guru or spiritual leaders were traditionally high-ranking Brahmins and part of a dominant caste system (Sarangapani, 2003). The guru ideal contributes to changing attitudes to teachers' roles in India. Due to technological advances and the wider reach of news through television in villages (Mooij, 2008), teachers are no longer sought as learned interpreters of the outside world. The cultural erosion of the teacher started during the British Raj where traditional gurus, respected for spiritual guidance and who led pious, simple lives, were employed as salaried teachers following the colonial education system (Mlecko, 1982; Sarangapani, 2003; Ganapathy-Coleman, 2014). Amu, Deepa, Celina and Bhargavi indirectly referenced guru-like respect and piety with contemporary Gandhian values of simplicity (Gupta, 2003; Thirumurthy et al, 2007; Joshi, 2009). The dominant focus of research on the guru is the 'guru–shishya' relationship – the teacher–student relationship.

Two studies examining the value orientations of Indian teachers position the teacher as a cultural symbol of moral restoration for traditional values eroded by globalisation (Kumar and Pandey, 2012; Triveni, 2014). In both studies, examining either teacher trainees' perceptions of values (Kumar and Pandey, 2012) or values of college teachers in the South Indian state of Karnataka (Triveni, 2014), researchers stated that as value education is expected of the Indian teacher, the issue was how to inculcate values into a young generation at risk of being lost to universal, global values that threaten indigenous values. Kumar and Pandey found teachers did conform to universal values of mutual respect and believed in open, balanced discussion with their students. The overall outcomes and analyses of both studies, however, reconstructed the teacher-disciple relationship, where the teacher acts as a guide to the wayward student needing such guidance to follow the 'correct' path.

The guru–shishya relationship depends on the commitment of the guru to the holistic development of the disciple, the shishya (Gupta,

2003; Sarangapani, 2003). It is a historical, cultural foundation for the teacher–student relationship found within contemporary teachers' responses in my research. In studies examining teachers' perceptions of their roles, teacher commitment to student learning is countered by expecting an equal commitment by the student to their academic achievement, made possible by submitting to the teacher's authority (Gupta, 2003; Sriprakash, 2011). The student is ultimately responsible for their academic underachievement because they have a choice to correct their behaviour and submit as a student-disciple or face potential failure.

Teacher authority is culturally embedded in teacher–student relationships and reinforced by parents. Parents from low-income backgrounds in an urban city in India demonstrated a high regard for teachers and saw their children as essentially naughty and distracted (Ganapathy-Coleman, 2014). Teachers enable students to achieve academically, including helping the immature child to mature into a responsible young adult, ready to engage in their family and social obligations. The teacher does all they can to help the student; not achieving this is placed on the student as a sign of immaturity and inherent misbehaviour. Education is thus a serious business with grave consequences for the student and their family if not followed appropriately. Teachers who are implicitly aware of this resort to government textbooks as a sole teaching aid (Vijaysimha, 2013) for fear of disrupting students' chances of achieving formal qualifications. This reveals the impact of neoliberal emphasis on achievement, especially at secondary school level, including teachers' awareness of the social realities that students will face once they leave the classroom.

This is also a continuation of teachers' caretaker and guide role, in which the teacher as guru prepares the student for their future based on what skills and knowledge the teacher feels the student needs. Whereas the traditional guru–shishya relationship was one based on spiritual guidance, the contemporary teacher–student relationship is driven by a need to prepare students for social and economic survival.

The guru–shishya relationship in education research is often called upon to explain or illustrate a socio-cultural background or context of education in India to outline the dominance of historical authoritative roles and as a symbol of prevalent structural hierarchies within India. The guru–shishya relationship certainly does highlight historical roots whose influence is extended to contemporary Indian society, but it falls short of adequately addressing wide-ranging sources of inequality, advocated by Feldman and Gellert (2006). It prioritises social structures of caste and gender within a traditional frame of reference in India. This restricts the examination of areas such as moral values and beliefs, including personal aspirations or an understanding of meaningful life. The guru serves as catch-all explanation for teacher identity within Indian education research, dominating perspectives for anyone seeking to understand how teachers approach their role outside of these dominant tropes.

There have been attempts to understand this tendency to reference the guru when describing the Indian teacher. Ganapathy-Coleman's (2014) study noted that parents recalled their own teachers with nostalgia and lamented their own misbehaviour in school. The nostalgia for one's teacher is linked to a cultural reference of the venerable guru but also a means of remembering one's childhood, of mediating memory to reconcile past with present. This reflective tool uses purposeful cultural references to put forward a sense of cultural authenticity, referring to a particular national and cultural identity (Ganapathy-Coleman, 2014). This was mainly employed by lower-class parents, as middle-class parents tend not to reference the cultural trope of the guru–shishya relationship. Referring to an idealised past, where the guru was a benevolent and spiritual caretaker of the disadvantaged, is a reminder of the failings of the current educational system and indicates widening social divides within the education system in India. My research aimed to understand what cultural references teachers used when describing their professional roles and what this could tell us about their values without the need to necessarily revert to a guru–shishya explanation, as has been done many times before. Examining cultural references without resorting to a direct and immediate reference to the guru can help us understand the Indian teacher in more depth if we further question 'how' and 'why' teachers express themselves in certain ways or use such cultural references.

Although there is a central concern with the guru as a catch-all explanation of the Indian situation, the guru as a symbol of care for the disadvantaged highlights how altruism, self-interest, emancipation and freedom of the teacher and student are approached in Indian literature. The teacher, recalling the guru's charity, contributes to the student's development defined by emancipation as freedom from restrictive structures or conditions such as poverty and social disadvantage (Giddens, 1991; Crocker, 1992). It is notable in the studies discussed in this section that possessing liberty of choice or freedom to make choices and decisions is rarely mentioned in a discussion of the teacher–student relationship. When it is referenced, it is a part of a discussion of social and economic aspirations in contradiction to teachers' emancipatory role (Mooij, 2008). This places the Indian teacher as a continual emancipator of the disadvantaged, reinforced by the cultural trope of the guru–shishya relationship. Therefore, it is important when examining teachers' responses that reference their altruistic act through their teaching to consider the role their gender plays within freedom of choice between themselves and their students. What freedom of choice is available to them as women and what role does gender play within this?

Role of gender in personal and professional aspirations

Gendered roles and markers such as marriage were used by teachers to describe who they were within their family as wife, mother, daughter, and sister. This set the framework from which their perspective and experience were described and explained.

As discussed earlier, Celina outlined her reason for joining the profession was due to her father losing his job, but family is underlined as being an important support for her when she herself lost her job,

Celina:	But so many times I've been fallen down, lifted up, fallen down, lifted up … it's all because my parents, my brother and sister they are the ones who motivated me when I was about to fall.
Researcher:	So family was very important?
Celina:	Family was very important for me.

Family is a crucial support system for Celina, who describes being "lifted up" by the unified force of parents, brother and sister who motivate her when she is "about to fall". The family provides support when she has fallen and through their encouragement prevents future falling. Celina made sacrifices in the past to support her family but they now support her, bringing about a sense of mutual support, especially in times of crisis. Celina's family helps maintain her role as a teacher and their joint effort continues to help her to recover and achieve, which she acknowledges as crucial for her recovery. She attributes her ability to overcome this to her family as reciprocal gratitude for their efforts. Her gendered role within the family is not made distinct, but forms part of a supportive family in which she as sister and daughter is supported.

This acknowledgement of family structures is prevalent in Bhargavi and Deepa's descriptions of their roles as daughter and wife in terms of their aspirations,

Bhargavi: More than 11 years ... soon after the marriage, I was working only for 3 years, I quit my job ... there in Peenya, after this school what I told you before ... there also 3 years I worked ... due to some problem the school was shut down ... then after marriage 3 years I was sitting idle at home, I was feeling very low so I requested so much my husband, then he allowed me to go for work. Just he was telling me, convincing me ... 'What is the use going for a job? Only we two are there, what you are going to do simply going to work?' ... But when you are feeling idle at home ... some value for education is there so I told better I go somewhere.

Bhargavi negotiated with her husband to start working after her marriage. Her husband's reasoning that her income is not needed illustrated her gendered role: her potential contribution to the family income is additional, as her role as wife and future mother is as beneficiary of her husband's earning capacity. Bhargavi's description of her husband's questions ("what are you going to do, simply going to work?") indicates a perception of work carried about by women as not having much significance apart from providing them with something to do to prevent the boredom of "sitting idle". Bhargavi's husband questions her logic by focusing on the act of going to work rather than the nature of work itself, indicating female-oriented professions are not seen as work, aligning with Ramachandran's (2000) work on perceptions of female work in India. Bhargavi seeks to explain her husband's reaction to her working. There is a clear emphasis on her husband's opposition, which she wins over by her main argument that she needs to get out of the house. Her value for education is placed second in her argument for being allowed to work. Bhargavi negotiates expectations of her role as wife and her need to work by conceding to her husband's perceptions to get the result she wants. It is this form of manoeuvring that helps define how women negotiate their aspirations: there is an awareness of how she will be perceived, including an understanding of how to work with such perceptions to achieve a result.

Deepa is distinct in outlining her future aspiration to continue with her education but points to her family obligations as structures that need to be maintained,

Researcher: Did you have any other ambition apart from being a teacher?

Deepa: Apart from being a teacher … actually I had, after my MSc, I want to do my PhD in Anatomy but after my marriage because of my personal problem, husband, wife, family … that is more responsibility than this problem. Because I want to … somewhat I have about the dead bodies, about something I want to study about dead bodies, what is there inside.

Researcher: Do you think you can still study?

Deepa: No, now I can't … because of the family, I cannot divert my mind anyway.

Researcher: I wish someday you will be able to do your PhD.

Deepa: No, that is impossible, I think so … before that marriage means my parents used to help so now responsibilities are more.

Deepa feels she is not able to do a doctorate as being a wife and daughter-in-law brought greater responsibility ("No, now I can't … because of the family, I cannot divert my mind anyway"). This references Deepa's prior descriptions of family life as a child in which she felt protected and looked after and where decisions and responsibility were taken away from her. On two separate occasions referring to her ambitions, she outlines her marriage as a key event that has disenabled her from achieving a doctorate.

Deepa states there is greater responsibility in her current life but does not allude to what these responsibilities are ("so now responsibilities are more"). This is passive acceptance of responsibilities that go along with being a wife but also deflection from getting too personal with the researcher, as a means of maintaining distance and protecting one's personal business from external scrutiny. Although Deepa was the more vocal of all teachers interviewed in talking about the impact her changing female role had on her ambitions, her reluctance to go into personal detail indicates a division between the internal world she inhabits with all her responsibilities and obligations that prevents her from going forward with her education, and the professional world that she is open to discuss. As with Bhargavi, how responses are framed and examples explained indicate that these women are aware of what is to be kept private and personal and what can be discussed with a stranger.

Statives of "because of my family, I cannot divert my mind away" serve as sufficient explanation for not being able to continue with her studies, which taps into a generic, accepted idea that "family" stands for a range of expected duties and responsibilities that prevent Deepa from stopping work and returning to education. Marriage indicates entry into adulthood and acceptance of duties, responsibilities and extended accountability to others apart from your parents and siblings. It is possible that, as a wife, returning to education redirects priorities away from the husband and his family to oneself and individual attainment.

Although keeping her role as wife separate from discussion, Deepa is more open to describing the maternal role she plays in the school,

Deepa: [B]ut outside, means after the class hour, I will be with them friendly, I used to share their feelings and I used to say the children 'Whatever is there, as a friend, as one like your mummy, you share with me, no problem. If I know I will give the suggestion, if I know I will give'.

Deepa's professional persona outside of teaching is to embody a maternal role, in which students can confide in her and she can continue her act of care by providing advice. Gupta's study (Gupta, 2003) on the maternal role of teachers sees the teacher extend her maternal role to her students. Deepa uses the role of a mother to demonstrate care to her students: she can help them beyond their academic lives and is invested emotionally in their lives as young people. She brings together professional and personal personas to put forward an image of herself as a teacher who goes beyond what is required as a classroom teacher and embodies characteristics of the mother/teacher in her interaction with students. Utilising a maternal role to show care for students uses gendered qualities or characteristics of a mother within the Indian context. In comparison to previous descriptions of a strict father, the mother embodies unconditional love and care. Deepa uses the mother to separate the friendly, approachable side of herself with the strict professional persona when interacting with students. This demonstrates an instinctive understanding of how female roles and figures are perceived, including using such characteristics for a particular purpose. Whatever personal aspirations Deepa has for her own role as a mother, using the maternal role within her professional context is crucial in understanding how teachers understand and utilise gender within their lives and aspirations.

In terms of the crossover between personal and professional contexts, Amu described how her role as a teacher filtered into her interaction with her children.

Amu: Yeah, I feel I became very rude. Even my family they tell me that … even my two daughters don't like the way I … the way I am here in the school, the same thing it has come out also … 'You are not a loving mum, you are very rude to us, you are very strict' and all … then I sit alone … when I go home, I think I shouldn't do this … but automatically when I see them doing something, no? I just burst out … sometimes I only feel I shouldn't do that.

Amu's children reacted negatively to her strict professional persona which she has expressed as a key teaching skill. Amu, by being made aware of how she is perceived, reflects upon this yet feels that her professional persona is so engrained in her that it is part of an instinctive reaction to situations ("I just burst out … sometimes I only feel I shouldn't do that"). The boundaries between personal and professional contexts are made porous in Amu's need to embody the strict disciplinarian persona of an effective teacher, in which she uses tone of voice and communication skills as defining factors. Amu's responses across her interviews emphasise the way she addresses students, whether it is how to question a student or her physical presence in a classroom. In comparison to Deepa, the mother/teacher role put across by Amu is less gentle and soft, inculcating aspects of her teaching style into her sense of self. Her roles as mother and teacher are combined and embedded in her daily interactions with both student and child.

Teachers' gendered role is defined through them being female in relation to someone. Their definition and description of their gendered experience are defined by their relationship to a husband, child or father, mother, brother or sister. Their gender mediates their relationships, their interactions and decisions to continue to work or study. As with their students, they share their aspirations with those to whom they are accountable or take care of, those who share ownership of their decisions, including their choice in being a teacher.

Shared ownership of knowledge and academic achievement

Sen (2005) views education as a means of actual freedom to enable individual choice, disallowing a single doctrine or dominant use within education. Actual freedom in the context of teachers interviewed is reworked to freedom that is guided and determined by teachers and parents.

As the individual is defined and shaped by their family and community, actual freedom as outlined by Sen may not be compatible with the way teachers view student learning and education. Sen sees the individual using knowledge gained from education to open greater possibilities for material prosperity and increasing capability. However, based on teachers' responses in my interviews, learning is an implicit and accepted set of negotiations between student, teacher and parent. Education as a commodity to provide greater choice and material prosperity may be useful as an ideal, but this concept needs to be adjusted in the face of education that reinforces asymmetric relationships between teacher/student and parent/child.

If student achievement is the joint effort of parent and teacher, student failure must also be addressed. In Morrow's (2013) study of young people who had failed their high school exams, student failure had consequences for their aspirations and sense of achievement, not just for themselves but for their family. In Amu's discussions of student failure, the student in question was described as not partaking in the joint effort by the teacher and school to help him succeed:

Amu: Yeah, we tried to do the same, the basic knowledge and all, so last year I think one child, he came from a different school actually … only for one year he was here, so we tried to do … even our head mistress … we all struggled with him and finally

> he started disturbing the other children ... taking the other children somewhere and roaming ... he was in 9th Standard, then the parents themselves took the TC and they went out and I heard that he's not ... complete the 10 Standard ... so with some private ... he's going to appear for the test ... through some other parents I heard.

Teachers struggling to help the student who disrupted other students' learning shows the student as not following teacher instruction and accepting help. The explanation that the student was due to complete their high school through private tuition indicates he was not compatible with the school's environment, in working with others or following rules. It is possible the student demonstrated an act of individual agency in not submitting to direction or sharing ownership of their education. That student in a sense exercised Sen's actual freedom, through continuing with their education outside of the school environment by alternative means that do not follow a single doctrine or dominant use. Student failure, as described by Amu, shows such students are incompatible with accepted implicit relationships between teacher and student. Student failure is also as an individual act, one in which rejection of joint effort breaks social relationships and leads to failure, and is primarily the student's responsibility.

The impact of student failure on teachers is indicated by Celina and Deepa. Celina reflects on student failure in a previous school as still affecting her sense of achievement:

Researcher: What about those cases when you couldn't get through to students?
Celina: Yes, two years back. Students failed, eight of them failed. I felt very bad. My value was not there. Because of those eight that failed, my entire value went down. I thought of searching for a job, my health is also very bad. I came here and found a job ... That is daily in my mind. That disappointment it is there, today also when I take the class, that time also I'll feel disappointed. Of course, why I feel disappointed is that I don't want to mess up anyone, distraction at home also, I'll feel disappointed. In the evening time, I used to take

> the tuitions, for first PUC [pre-university college], I've taken, second PUC I've taken, BCom I've taken … tuitions. It was cooperative from their side and I used to teach them and bring them to the right path. That was my case.

Celina saw the failure of eight students as reducing her sense of value and being a source of continued disappointment in her teaching. Student failure is not strictly individual action: it is one of rejecting joint effort with the teacher, which makes it complex when that joint effort does not result in success. Interestingly, this incident does not precipitate Celina to question her methods or relationship with students; she offers examples of where she was successful in individual private tuitions with students from higher levels ("It was cooperative from their side and I used to teach them and bring them to the right path. That was my case"). In stating "why I feel disappointed is that I don't want to mess up anyone", Celina articulates her disappointment in affecting the students' chances to lead a successful life. The alternative impact of the teacher upon her student's achievement is not always a positive relationship in which achievement is confirmed, but one in which the teacher and student are tied together and in which both impact each other. The asymmetrical relationship between teacher and student is balanced in student failure. It is within these situations that relationships and implicit forms of negotiation are looked at by the teacher.

Collective achievement through student affirmation and acknowledgement

Sen's 'human development paradigm/capability approach' and Nussbaum's 'central human capabilities' (Sen, 1997, 2005; Nussbaum, 1999, 2007, 2009; Anand and Sen, 2000) outlined a set of predefined values as influencing middle-class aspirations and refocusing education policy in India to promote a global, English-speaking population (Mooij, 2008; Morrow, 2013; Robinson-Pant and Singal, 2013a). Sen's capability approach placed education as key to an individual's productivity and material prosperity, indirectly contributing to economic stability and social development. Building on human capability, Nussbaum's cross-cultural norms, through a set of predefined central human capabilities, attempted to protect political liberty and choice.

This research found that predefined values of academic achievement emerged from teachers' discussions. Student achievement enabled an accepted pathway of high school exam performance, further and higher education and choice of profession determined by a student's parents and family.

Education as a route out of poverty through personal productivity and social contribution was reflected in teachers' responses that emphasised communal effort towards collective emancipation. Communal effort towards collective emancipation is drawn from teachers' experiences and descriptions. This research does not infer whether this is right or wrong, but is part of analysis pertaining to concepts that may underpin teacher values.

Research findings differed from an understanding of achievement as a product of individual work and capability (Sen, 2005) to one that is the outcome of the collective, communal effort between teacher and student, parent, and child. Social, economic and political factors were not given as much prominence by teachers as the family and teacher in ensuring student achievement. The success of a student was both due to their hard work and a product of teacher and parent investment. Student achievement brought about social development not only for themselves but for their family, placing pressure on students to bring themselves and their families out of poverty.

This relates to Morrow's study on aspirations of young people in Andhra Pradesh who failed to get onto further education and university pathways (Morrow, 2013). Morrow found the pressures on young people to perform well at summative examinations was one of mutual obligation to help emancipate their family through education; this defined their individual choice and aspirations. This was reflected in teachers' descriptions of their childhood and parental influence in deciding their own further and higher education routes. Bhargavi and Celina spoke of family obligations to take up teaching to provide financial assistance when their parents were unable to work.

Mutual obligation between parent and child, student and family differ from Giddens' avocation of life politics as individual emancipation from traditional, restrictive structures where one possesses the freedom to choose one's lifestyle and develop an individual morality of authenticity through continual self-discovery (Giddens, 1991). Giddens' morality of authenticity, that maintains being true to the individual self, is made complex given the dominance of family and social ties within teachers' reflections. A child's academic success helps place them and their families on the path to possessing greater choice in affording commodities and higher social standing, redefining a morality of authenticity centred on mutuality of purpose between individual and family.

Emancipation, for teachers, is distinctly economic where social emancipation is not apparent nor individual self-discovery applicable. To think and operate as a collective, to help one's family out of poverty, demonstrates gratitude to one's parents and acknowledges their hard work in investing in their education and upbringing. This was referred to by teachers in descriptions of expected student behaviour to parents and themselves. Reciprocal duty of care to one's family is actioned through alleviating future financial burden. This reinforces social cohesion and family relation and reciprocates in part the effort of one's family to raise children to succeed, a sentiment echoed by teachers in their own descriptions of responsibilities to their students.

A culture of individual self-discovery leading to emancipation is challenging in this context, as the individual operates within collective social ties and obligations. It is not as straightforward to extricate oneself from such collective contexts as it may be within individual-focused, liberal societies. The traditional ascetic within Hindu culture may opt out of society and reject material concerns in their spiritual quest for nirvana. The difference between self-discovery as espoused by Giddens and that of the traditional ascetic is that the ascetic rejects social and economic concerns altogether; for the ascetic, self-discovery is geared towards bodily control to attain spiritual enlightenment, with social restrictions as a part of mortal, earthly concerns.

Economic emancipation within a context of collective emancipation may make it more difficult to rise out of poverty. However, as outlined by teachers' descriptions of their role, social cohesion and reciprocal care acknowledge those who contribute towards this route out of poverty, the teacher's and parents' hard work in supporting the student as part of collective achievement and emancipation, mediated by expected teacher–student relationships and passive student action.

Implications for reflective practice for teacher education
Social relationships and teachers' perceptions

Social relationships between teacher and student, and parent and student underpinned how teachers viewed their role. These views contributed to an understanding of their values within this.

Collective achievement and emancipation within the teacher–student relationship are bound by values based on a teacher's care for their students and student acknowledgment of such care. Care and gratitude are central to the teacher's role and their relationships with students. This is particularly evident when dealing with student failure. External explanations for student failure, such as ill health, indicate the vulnerable position teachers feel they are in, in relation to student achievement. Given the context of communal achievement, the need to protect one's reputation and efficacy reveals the pressures teachers feel to perform as well as their students. It may also help illustrate the need for teachers to place prime responsibility for failure on students themselves, to disassociate from an individual rogue student, and to reaffirm their effectiveness and authority within the school and among colleagues.

Teacher values based on social relationships are defined by collective effort, aspirations, understanding of achievement and a demonstration of care by the teacher to the grateful student. Within these, asymmetrical relationships operate as both student and teacher are dependent on the other either to provide learning for future achievement or confirm professional efficacy through academic achievement and direct verbal acknowledgment. Teacher values surrounding emancipatory obligations define parent–child relationships in ways that teachers experienced themselves as children

Table 2.1: Teachers' perceptions of their role in relation to reflective practice in teacher education

Teachers' perceptions of their role: *Value of social relationships*	Teacher–student relationships	Reflective practice in teacher education
	Moral, altruistic purpose of teaching that prioritises teacher action over passive student action	Teacher training could benefit from examining duty of care within specific role and responsibilities during placement or in-service practice
		The teacher's voice can extend beyond instruction or discipline to building effective social relationships with students
	Communal achievement and collective emancipation	Reflective practice in teacher education
	Teachers' gendered family and social obligations that define their personal and professional aspirations	Examining situations or issues that are not directly related to teachers could help them approach and engage with their own values

and carry with them into their relationships with students. Social relationships prioritise the collective and communal, in which teachers, students, parents, and their children interact and negotiate their individual selves. What is interesting about the context in which social relation values arise among teachers' perceptions of their role is that it is defined by a need to maintain social cohesion within communities and groups.

Social relationships and implications for reflective practice

Examining social relationships between students and their families can provide an external frame from which teachers could examine their own attitudes to student achievement and aspirations. Trainee teachers could engage with underlying values in relation to issues of achievement, success, and family and social obligations. It may not be possible for teachers directly to self-examine or identify their values within this context, but through the prism of examining family pressure and obligations on student success, teachers can indirectly examine their attitudes to these external factors and the values that underwrite it. This greater awareness has the potential to enable teachers to engage with their own experiences and instigate a reflective process for them.

Teacher education programmes could examine the teacher–student relationship in relation to success and failure. Programmes can look at the duty of care and expectations of teachers as understood by teachers themselves. Through examining care within their teaching, teachers could look at their role as educators and carers in the classroom, aspects in which learning and care are entangled and implicit within their interaction with students (see Table 2.1).

Training could examine expected duties and values that govern teachers' understanding of their role and responsibilities. This could help develop greater understanding of how care and learning are related and linked to teaching. By emphasising the duty of care within the classroom, teachers are enabled to explicate the type of care that supports learning that is specific to their classroom environment and their students. Teachers are able to have a more informed understanding of this aspect of their role, which is implicit and assumed but not specifically supported with regard to the unique contexts in which they teach.

Social relation values can help training programmes highlight the role of speech as a key instrument and resource for teachers to maintain key social relationships within their professional practice, such as those with their students, colleagues and parents. The particularity of speech is significant for training programmes to enable a deeper understanding. Examining how one speaks to another can support teachers' definitions of themselves, their roles and how these definitions direct and impact their interaction with students and their learning. Being made more aware of the way one speaks could tap into a key resource that teachers rely upon within the classroom but that could also act as a means toward reflection on the technical use of one's voice and speech.

A focus on speech can highlight the significance of verbal communication within training programmes as going beyond a teaching technique to communicate to students to become a way to understand oneself. Trainee teachers could benefit from acknowledging the specific space of using their voice. Teachers' descriptions centre upon their voice to command or encourage students. Training could consider looking at the teacher's voice as one that constructs relationships with students. This could cover tone, intonation and spoken syntax to align with intended action of both the teacher and student.

This emphasis on the teacher's voice can also help feed into the oral tradition of India and be a main teaching tool used by teachers in schools with limited teaching resources. Given the social context, self-identification and evaluation may require looking at how teacher and student interact through verbal interaction of instruction and response. Examining the performance of teaching through verbal dialogue and interplay can help teachers understand how one's voice is used to teach and enact social relationships with students, and how this can be beneficial for their teaching.

3

Teachers' perspectives on navigating social spaces

This chapter analyses the way female teachers navigated internal and external social spaces in their responses (see Figure 3.1). Teachers were careful in how they framed their responses and reconstructed their spoken sentences to questions relating to other schools, external communities or the internal school community to which they belong.

The process by which transcripts were coded through data analysis tools provides a key introduction to agency through speech within this chapter. Social languages and situated meaning outline stages of data analysis that significantly contributed to a deeper understanding of how teachers reconstructed their speech to navigate between social spaces. These include how teachers described mediating gendered spaces and the role language plays in their use of language to navigate internal and external social spaces. The chapter concludes with implications for reflective practice in teacher education.

Social languages and situated meaning

The concepts of social languages and situated meaning formed the basis for initial analysis of transcripts. The social languages tool put forward by Gee (2011) helped our understanding of how words, phrases, clauses

Figure 3.1: Chapter 3 outline

and sentences indicate a social language that may be constructed from more than one national language. This helped this analysis of teacher responses that combine Indian language sentence structure with English vocabulary. The concept of situated meanings emphasises meanings attributed to words and phrases and the context that is constructed. Given teachers' use of description and metaphor, this tool was useful to understand different meanings associated with terms and phrases.

Syntax and intonation of speech were used to examine individual interviews and group discussions. Syntax included sentence structure, topicalisation, left and right dislocation (LD and RD) and elliptical repetition as initial codes (Lange, 2012). Intonation examined oral emphasis placed on certain sections of speech in which the 'pitch-glide' of speech is noted. When speaking, the way one's voice rises and falls, or falls and rises ('rise-fall' or 'fall-rise'), indicates the ending or beginning of an 'idea-unit' (Gee, 2011). They act as verbal markers of the beginning or end of a point or statement being made. Lange's syntax structure, with topicalisation and left and right dislocation, relates to Gee's intonation tool of 'pitch-glide', with the beginning and ending of an 'idea-unit'. For example, if a teacher states, 'I will talk, they will listen', the teacher is active at the top of the sentence with the student as passive at the end of the sentence, which correlates to the pitch-glide of the sentence when spoken.

Listening back to oral recordings along with the written transcript was invaluable within this process. The written words of the teacher combined with listening to the rise-fall/fall-rise of their speech could only ever be analysed in conjunction with each other and not separately. This gave a unique richness to the data collected, as did the distinctive spoken syntax of the teachers being interviewed. Syntax and intonation tools of inquiry were therefore combined to facilitate a broader scope for data analysis (see Figure 3.2).

Following initial data analysis, a matrix of key findings and related codes was put together. Initial codes of topicalisation and and pitch-glide developed into three main areas of sentence structure, positioning opinion and researcher-teacher relationship. A summary of the key findings is shown in Tables 3.1 and 3.2. Transcripts were analysed line by line and outlined as sentence level or the stanza level indicated by macro level. Active and passive language were used to indicate intonation and emphasis placed by the teacher, and where the idea-unit ended or began during each sentence or stanza.

Figure 3.2: Outline of mixed/multi-method approach and data analysis tools of inquiry development

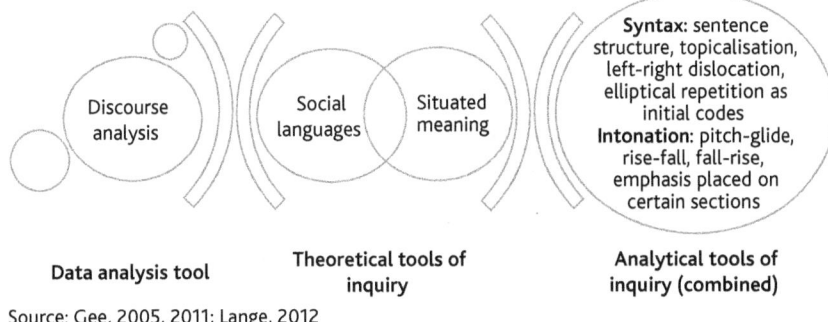

Source: Gee, 2005, 2011; Lange, 2012

This data analysis was designed to bring forward mechanisms used in speech not only to form and maintain social relationships but also to locate the speaker within a group or, at times, remove themselves from representing their group's shared views. This chapter will focus on the ways teachers navigated these social spaces by examining not just what they said but how they spoke.

Mediating gendered spaces through group consensus

As with the teacher–student relationship, performing expected roles is prevalent among teachers. In group discussions, teachers responded to questions as a group, with group consensus a key aspect of their relationship.

Group discussions were conducted within the two schools in which the interviewed teachers taught, with one group per school. Each group included teachers individually interviewed and observed, with two additional teachers from the same school to act as a focus group. Group 1 consisted of Amu and Bhargavi plus teachers Gayatri and Roopa. Group 2 had Celina and Deepa plus teachers Lakshmi and Savitri. First, teachers were asked to look at two scenarios involving hypothetical situations of two students in pairs and then feed back to the rest of group. Second, all teachers were asked to look at a scenario involving a hypothetical situation of a new teacher at their school. Group consensus was observed when elliptical repetition, in which group members' repeated phrases ("so easy", "compared to other") were used to show agreement and unity.

Table 3.1: Detail from syntax intonation data analysis matrix (a)

Level	Active	Passive
_____		
LD to RD syntax–sentence structure		
Sentence	Teacher action	Student reciprocal action
Macro	Statement	Explanation
Macro	Narrative	Statement
Sentence	See/means	Explanation
Sentence	External Force – bring/push	Statement
Macro	Past – used to be	Now – present
Macro	Cause	Effect
Macro	Cause	Reversal/upending order
	Passive	**Active**
Sentence	Negative inversion	Student/teacher action
Macro	Humility/modesty	Assertive – can do/ability
Sentence	Accepting uncertainty	Internal strength – readiness
Positioning opinion		
Sentence	Assertive positioning: in my opinion/actually/according to me	Statement/opinion
Sentence	Defensive positioning: I am not saying/not like that	Statement opinion
Sentence	Verbal parenthesis – not like that	Further clarification/qualifying statement
Sentence	Non-specific references	Avoidance
Macro	Acceptance of reality	Placing into wider context as justification
Participant–researcher relationship		
Sentence	Elliptical repetition	Continued response
Macro	Free movement SOV/SVO	Linguistic negotiation

Group 2

Lakshmi: The responsibility on us that we are giving a good education to our future, that is.
Deepa: That is not so easy.
Lakshmi: So easy job, ma'am.
Deepa: Compared to other jobs.
Lakshmi: Compared to others.

Table 3.2: Detail from syntax intonation data analysis matrix (b)

Key finding-code: social languages – syntax	Examples	Description/analysis: Building task: significance – practice	Significance for research
LD-RD sentence structure: **Code LD (active) to RD (passive)** *Teacher action to student Reciprocal action* Level: sentence/clause	Amu: Yeah … first and foremost. See we have to bring all their attention to us, the concentration so to not even one child should not peep through a window or somewhere. So first the way I output, everybody will be on my side. Bhargavi: What I think is … whatever I want to teach the students, they should say "OK, this teacher she has taught us in a very nice way, it is very interesting". I want always to have an interaction with the students in such a way that they should understand each and everything what I say.	Teacher action is given priority and topicalised to the opening, the left of sentences/clauses. Student reciprocal action is placed at the end, dislocated to the right of sentences/clauses. Teacher action/thought is active while student action/thought is passive. Process/sequence: teacher action directly influences student action – active force on passive acceptance.	Way participants see their role as educators - description of duty – left to right – active to passive Hierarchy of teacher–student relationship – positional authority Possible relationship to teaching style in classroom Form of distributed personhood – student a recipient and future actor of teacher's personhood – knowledge/value systems Reveal attitudes to choice/freedom and capability
Code: LD (active) to RD (passive) *Statement to example as explanation* Level: macro/stanza	Celina: By asking them questions, directly I ask them, sometimes, what happens, for example, notes is there, **the child is a very naughtiest child in the class, if you feel. If you can make that small child to come to the board and write.** Actively it is given to that person to engage in some work, making him to engage in some work. I am doing something with the other students, so this person is distracting, so the distracting person should be brought to the concentration of the class.	Statement is made at the beginning of a stanza followed by an example or illustration of how the teacher puts this into action. The opening statement or response is often an elliptical sentence followed by a detailed example that stands in for analysis. Process/sequence: definitive statement followed by explanation. Active statement to passive explanation.	Can be related to teaching style of making a definitive statement followed by explanation as a means of qualifying the statement Example standing in for analysis can reveal attitudes to assumed knowledge/understanding Reliance on narrative/story acting as explanation – limiting analysis? Focus on HOW not WHY

Note: bold in the examples indicates left/right dislocation

Group 1

Researcher:	How will you help them? Would you go into their class and see how they teach? Or talk to them afterwards?
Amu:	Yeah, afterwards … in the class we can't go do that.
Gayatri:	After the class.
Bhargavi:	After the class hours whenever.

The need to maintain consensus through repeating each other's responses puts forward a unified response to myself as outsider. The relationship among teachers is one of mutual affirmation and support. Within the scenarios, the teacher is expected to share their knowledge and experience to outline expected student behaviour and action. The process of sharing individual knowledge came together as a group response, strengthened by elliptical repetition. This demonstrates a need for cohesiveness, of a shared sense of identity as part of a teaching community. Group 1's responses to a scenario involving a newly qualified teacher, who struggled in their first few weeks, demonstrates elliptical repetition or building on each other's responses.

Roopa:	Tell her to dedicate her work … because teacher's job is not so easy … it's very difficult to handle children so we'll tell her to dedicate her work, first of all and if she'll really dedicate her work, she'll not have that fear of teaching and she'll be very kind to all the students … ok?
Bhargavi:	She'll be free of mind … first thing basically she has to understand she has to learn to adjust with the students, know what are the basic things so that being a friendly way.
Amu:	We have to convince her first … like what is our experience.
Bhargavi:	Be very straight with the students.
Roopa:	That's what we'll advise her to dedicate.
Bhargavi:	Try to do that one.
Roopa:	First thing is, to dedicate her work.
Amu:	No, once she gets used to the children, she will understand.
Bhargavi:	She will understand.

Amu:	And we tell her own experience ... even we have come here for teaching, how kind we are to the children so definitely she will change herself and one, she will enjoy teaching also, once she can cope. See, all kinds of childrens [sic] are there ... not only everybody are troublesome ... some are very ...
Roopa:	Some are very good children.
Bhargavi:	Some are mischievous are there.
Amu:	So she will enjoy everything so ... when they are weak also, there she can concentrate more, if they are very talented.
Gayatri:	Seeing other teachers, she will change herself once she'll concentrate on her teaching.

Teachers defined their group identity through shared suggestions and elliptical repetition supporting each other when questioned by myself (Roopa: That's what we'll advise her to dedicate. Bhargavi: Try to do that one. Roopa: First thing is, to dedicate her work. Amu: No, once she gets used to the children, she will understand. Bhargavi: She will understand). Teachers came together to educate and inform me of their combined knowledge of teacher expectations. Consensus on what was the right way to approach the issue was important to maintain their unity and community. Consensus and agreement among teachers unified their professional community, providing a communal identity underlined by a unified sense of agency in which the teacher acts as part of a group. This can support how reflective practice may need to account for communal identity when seeking individual reflection towards professional development.

Acting as a group to ensure a particular outcome was observed in group responses to the scenario involving an underperforming student. 'Asha' was a final year, Standard 10 student who had decided to leave school to pursue her dancing career. Group 1 insisted that Asha needed to complete her high school education before she went ahead with her dancing career, whereas Group 2 indicated it was possible to continue with her career if she can balance the demands of school.

Group 1

Amu:	Yeah, so this is what as a subject teacher, we all will concentrate on her, each of us will tell so

	she thinks 'Oh everybody are ... everybody's thinking is same so why don't me also do that?' So definitely she will change her mind, we'll speak to her parents and her sister.
Gayatri:	Her sister.
Amu:	So they see somehow that she has to take up the exam.

Group 2

Savitri:	We decided let her continue in her career in dance only.
Deepa:	Dance only ... let she continue.
Savitri:	Let her do both the sides ... dance and study.
Researcher:	So you're entitled to do whatever you wish to get done, but after school?
Deepa:	Not after the school, not what I'm telling ... let she concentrate in studies also ... undertake other ways ... she can go to any friend's house, or any good teacher ... she can take it and she can.
Researcher:	So if she says 'I want to leave school ...'
Savitri:	No, no.
Deepa:	No, no ... no need to leave the school, 10th standard is not so difficult ... she can ...
Researcher:	She can still do her exams?
Deepa:	She can do her exams, she can pass.
Savitri:	She must focus on both sides ... balance.
Researcher:	Who will provide her that balance?
Deepa:	Parents.
Savitri:	Parents and teachers ... both also.

Group 1 put forward teacher action as group action to ensure that the student continued their education through their ability to convince the student's parents and family ("we all will concentrate on her, each of us will tell so she thinks 'Oh everybody are ... everybody's thinking is same so why don't me also do that?' So definitely she will change her mind, we'll speak to her parents and her sister"). For Group 2, group action was the combined effort of the teacher and parent to support thffectnt's ability to balance aspiration and education (Savitri: She must focus on both sides ... balance. Researcher: Who will provide her that balance? Deepa: Parents. Savitri: Parents and teachers ... both also.)

Group 1 were part of a school run by female management and teachers in which there was a strong sense of gendered community, whereas Group 2's school was run by male management and mainly female teachers. The suggestion to influence the student and parents by Group 1 indicates teachers acting together to fulfil objectives. Group 2's relationships with each other are tempered by their need to maintain reality in their response. Group consensus is redefined through a shared awareness of needing to be flexible and respond to change rather than prevent it. Despite the variance in response, group consensus among both groups worked to provide a solution that ensured learning was met. The value of education, and their role within it, was not compromised in either response.

Socially accepted spaces for female teachers

Group discussions with teachers and their peers included a discussion on why the teaching profession may be suitable for women. Group 1 put forward two main reasons as convenience and comfort in working in a female-oriented environment.

Researcher:	You mentioned for ladies this job is good, why is that?
Roopa:	Why means … teaching is more … ladies will be there and we'll be very convenient to talk with them and mingle with them … office means more gents, more men will be there and we'll not mingle so much.
Bhargavi:	Also office timings are not so convenient for us … we'll go in the morning, working till evening 6, 7 sometimes, we'll be drawn into that also … so it is not so convenient, here in schools and all we have our proper timings. We enjoy almost for each and every benefits here in the schools and for coming about teaching across to teachers … what we don't' know also … just going through different, each and every five years, the syllabus keep on changing, we come to know across many new things, even though we have studied but in some cases we didn't … it is not that we know everything.

Roopa outlines the key difference between a school and office environment is the dominance of women in the teaching profession. A woman, especially if she is married, does not traditionally associate or form relationships with men apart from those with familial connections. Mixed gendered environments such as offices are spaces in which such relationships have potential to be formed and pose difficulties for women who are increasingly aware of how they might be perceived by fellow colleagues and their families ("office means more gents, more men will be there and we'll not mingle so much" [Bhargavi]). In negotiating perceptions of others and guarding against misrepresentation, female-oriented professions that are acceptable within their social systems are chosen. In addition to the socially accepted maternal role of the teacher previously discussed, teaching is more convenient for the teacher to continue to take care of their family as the working day is shorter. In contrast, Group 2 discusses the convenience of being a teacher but does not agree that it is any more convenient than any other profession:

Researcher:	What about convenience? For example, the hours that you finish at 3:30 allows you to go your family, allows you to work in a place where you are not in an office, you are not coming late at night, what about convenience sake?
Celina:	Teacher's job is a convenient job which I feel.
Savitri:	It is a convenient job.
Researcher:	Is it safe like that, in that sense?
Deepa:	Convenient is … how we will make life like convenient … suppose I go to other job, I can make it satisfactory to my house and I can. That is according to our lifestyle … convenient … if I do, okay, this is 3:30, 3:30 I'm going back so whatever the timings of the work, I can do. Suppose I'm going to any company, according to that situation I will adjust.
Celina:	Environment makes you to mould your situation.
Deepa:	So, I won't say teacher job is a convenient job and so easy job, no … very tough job.

Deepa rejects the idea that teaching holds any convenience apart from being a profession with different working hours. There is no specific mention of gender in this discussion. Being a working woman is not specified as it is with Group 1. Celina's statement that one's environment "makes you to mould your situation" indicates an approach where one adjusts to professional environments and circumstances.

Group 1 states that teaching allows women a certain freedom to mingle in their work environment. This expresses a stronger sense of communal identity as female teachers and not limited to being a wife, mother or daughter to someone else. It is not an externally defined relationship but internal and homogenous, allowing for reduction of at least one structural hierarchy between genders. Teaching facilitates their roles as wives and mothers and is considered convenient, but also provides a space in which they can partake in shared experiences. In contrast, Group 2's promotion of moulding oneself indicates their perception of professional spaces as needing to be negotiated and adjusted to, that it is their role as workers to adjust to their environment and accommodate to what is given to them.

There are further distinctions. Group 1 sees their profession as supporting being a wife and mother. It allows them to work with other women to avoid mingling with men in office spaces and return home in time to look after the family, which may include extended family members. They are more active in descriptions of teaching and the way they negotiate expectations. They are the main actors within their sets of obligations and social systems. Group 2, in adjusting and moulding to situations or environments, puts across a more passive outlook in which they do still negotiate expectations. But, for them, teaching is not necessarily as safe and comfortable a space as for Group 1. It is like any other profession in which hours are adjusted to and personal circumstances altered.

In relation to a collective identity based on profession, gender allows for female teachers to enable a sense of communal identity far greater than that of being a teacher. Being a female teacher places gender as going beyond defining aspirations and social relationships to forming a sense of communal identity in which women are strengthened and made to feel more active in their implicit decisions and choices.

Maintaining social spaces: what a meaningful life is for teachers

Teachers' responses to what a meaningful life is, for themselves and their students, revealed a need to maintain social cohesion by avoiding conflict within their community and social spaces.

The main element of central human capabilities (CHC) (Nussbaum, 1999, 2007, 2009) is based on the key principle of what is needed for individuals to live happy and healthy lives. Teachers' beliefs referred to values of health and happiness rather than stipulating social, economic or political requirements.

Deepa approaches this from a child's perspective, pointing to the need for healthy food and shelter provided by one's parents. Happiness is a result of the security provided by parents who shield the child from their worries and provide guidance and discipline within the home environment,

Deepa: Healthy and happy wise ... according to me, my opinion ... main thing is good healthy food, healthy means not delicious food ... good food and good shelter to live ... not like bungalow style ... and happy life means ... the parents ... for example, children needs good parents, good parents means like good guidance they don't know, they also have done some mistake but some parents are, 'My child should not do like this, my child should not behave like what I have done ... my child should not do' ... parents who are not well educated, I will say ... good background people I will say ... this is mainly for one small shelter and food and happy life.

Researcher: And a happy life that comes from your parents?

Deepa: Yes, happy life will come ... because they won't have also, they won't show their difficulties to us, they will be happy for whatever I can give my child, they will provide ... not protection, obviously that will be ... for example, I will ask one ball, but I will ask like INR 100 ball, my parents cannot, but they will provide me INR 10 ball ... providing is there, they will do their duty, parents will.

Bhargavi stresses the need for being honest and truthful in achieving happiness, rejecting material happiness in favour of being grateful for what is God-given, as a marker of gratitude and being content with their lives. Bhargavi places her beliefs as central to her understanding of a meaningful life, in which she is ultimately grateful for being blessed with family and security:

Researcher: In your opinion, what is the main things one needs to lead a healthy and a happy life?

Bhargavi: They should have a good heart, pure in heart, having truth in the heart, ok? Whatever they speak they should do that one, ok … not something having some inferior complex … keeping something inside the mind and saying something outside … ok. I hate such type of person and I too don't have that kind of habit … double game … whatever I say, I do that one … what comes within my heart … I speak to the children … straightforward … I don't like talking in front one and at the back one … I hate all this.

Researcher: What about things, do you need to have cars, a house? Do those things mean happiness?

Bhargavi: Not at all, true happiness is when you are peaceful in the heart, you know. That is the true happiness, we get, what God has given … everyday we pray for God that only, give me peace of mind to me, so that I can stay happily … whether you have given me everything in my life or not … I have a good husband, good children he has given me … whatever I need, never in my life I dreamt of having those bungalows, cars anything never … whatever God has given me, up till now, really I am very thankful to him and very happy.

Celina and Deepa, like Bhargavi, focus on internal qualities of peace and having a peaceful mind. Celina outlines that a peaceful mind enables achievement by not being disturbed by others and living a life involving family, friends and living for oneself:

Researcher: You mentioned to lead a human life, you need certain things … What is needed for anyone in the world to lead a healthy and happy life?

Celina: Peace … Peaceful mind. Distraction, disturbances, criticision [sic] by the opposite party will not

> lead you a happy life. When you have a peaceful mind, otherwise you can achieve, otherwise you can never achieve anything. I went through so many disturbances, I'm ok now but ... through God's grace with the help I got from [lists schools worked in] it made me to mould myself. I have learnt a lesson from each student of the different schools. Learning a lesson is important, it is not in preparing for the teaching, it is not that. Somebody falls down in their studies, you need to rise up, you need to assess the child again.

Amu reiterates Bhargavi's emphasis on the need to be left alone by others, pointing to personal satisfaction, and not being criticised and interfered with.

Researcher: What do you think the central human capabilities, the things we need in all our lives to live a healthy, happy life?

Amu: That is ... we should be satisfied and whatever we think ... at least 60 to 70 per cent we must be satisfied. Once what you want you're not getting and forcibly we are doing some things, ok ... some satisfaction, you think I come to school to achieve ... here if I am not able to freely not able to teach them, so then you think 'Can I have a peace of mind?' that worries me ... that worries and I can't concentrate ... moreover even my health will go down ... satisfaction and peace of mind should be there which permits me to do my work peacefully ... every now and then somebody coming and disturbing us and what I am doing they say 'That is wrong, you do this' ... so that way and all, it disturbs.

Although differing on whether it comes from material security, personal values of truth and honesty or the need not to be criticised, teachers emphasised the need for peace of mind (see Figure 3.3). Deepa's need to protect a child from worry is taken on by parents ("providing is there, they will do their duty, parents will"). Bhargavi

Figure 3.3: Key elements of maintaining peace of mind based on responses

- Satisfaction with what one has
- Parents providing food and shelter
- Not contesting criticism from others
- Maintaining internal peace of mind

outlined personal values of truth and honesty to maintain peace of mind, not to live a dubious or deceitful existence and to be grateful for what God has provided ("everyday we pray for God that only, give me peace of mind to me, so that I can stay happily"). Celina and Amu are clearer in distinguishing external disruptions that affect their achievement or sense of satisfaction taking place through external criticism of their work or themselves.

This focus on internal calm or peace by teachers indicates the need for isolation, to be away from external disturbances, which may also indicate a need to be separated from social obligations ("every now and then somebody coming and disturbing us and what I am doing they say 'That is wrong, you do this' … so that way and all, it disturbs" [Amu]). This desire to be left alone could be a way for teachers to express their agentive freedom to exit social relationships (de Herdt and Bastiaensen, 2008; Burkitt, 2016).

Amu and Celina point to others interfering or criticising them as something that causes them worry and anxiety, disrupting their happiness. These criticisms are not opposed or contested but put up with, contributing to an internal desire to being left alone. Teachers may have been referring to criticism from those in positions of authority to them, both professionally and personally, outlining difficulties they find themselves in when encountering negative social interactions. They do not enact upon or isolate themselves but leave others to do so to them. They do not jeopardise their relationships with their critics through contesting or exiting relationships but instead develop a desire for isolation without demonstrating agency to answer their critics or separate themselves.

This is to maintain social relationships by not breaking or ending the relationship themselves.

In emphasising personal values of health, happiness and its relational component, teachers' understanding of CHC indicates a desire for avoiding conflict through being truthful and not being exposed to negative social relation. By looking at what they understand of conflict, it may be possible to understand what a meaningful life for teachers and their students is and how it relates to ways they navigate their internal and external social spaces.

Teacher views on conflict

So, as outlined, teachers focused on peace of mind as a foundation for happiness. To understand further their views on what constitutes a meaningful life, it is important to consider what is seen to threaten it.

In teachers' descriptions of an issue or problem, the cause is often external to the teacher, caused by something outside their domain. Amu and Bhargavi refer to parents' involvement with their children as affecting their ability to perform well in exams or in deciding their children's future. Deepa was more vocal about what constituted conflict in descriptions of problems with parents:

Deepa: 'Who are you?' they will argue … especially in this locality … Tamilians … they are the fighters … really I'm telling you … don't feel bad … they don't know what's going on … 'OK, the teacher has told … why have they told?' they are thinking 'Who are they to tell? I have given birth … I'm the parent, I am paying the fees, who is she, who is he?' Like that they do … they won't think as our parents did 'Teacher scolded, I will come next day to complain more about you' … our parents used to say … Nowadays, many teachers for their duty they will come, they will teach and they will go … because of this.

Deepa's perceived disrespect from parents is linked to underlying cultural difference between the local population and immigrant population of Tamilians from the neighbouring state of Tamil Nadu. The problem does not lie with her interaction with them, but their interaction with her ("they are the fighters"). They bring conflict and do not support the traditional role of the teacher and their authority. This is both an issue with lack of parental support as well as a cultural stereotype of Tamilians, who are considered louder than gentle-speaking Kannadigas. The questioning of parents by asking 'Who are you?' or 'Who are they to tell?' draws together the central issue Deepa has with these parents, that they question her status and identity among her students and subsequently in relation to them. Their cultural outsider status contributes further to this lack of recognition.

Celina, in contrast, views problems as arising from student action in looking for easier ways to study:

Celina: Nowadays, the students are not studying a textbook, the author has been putting his effort in order to write and explain, people are not going for the textbook. They are not reading the work. Instead, they are going for the supplementary books which guides them. It helps them, but what is the value of the author then? The person has researched so much, writes so many theses. His effort is not valued with some other guides. They want supplementary, that means the work is not suitable for their studies.

Researcher: Is it the parents who are buying these?

Celina: It is not the parents, the study of the textbook, when they find the difficulties in that, to cope up with that, they are going to supplementary.

Celina points to study supplements and guides rather than the main textbook being taught by the teacher. Celina states this devalues the work of textbook authors, as a form of disrespect to their hard work and research ("It helps them, but what is the value of the author then?"). In addition to the student's choice to use study guides, it is the guides themselves that cause conflict by offering an easier and unsuitable option for students, who use specific information and phrases to pass exams.

With Celina and Deepa, there is frustration with those who do not follow a set system, either with parents responding appropriately to a teacher's discipline of their child or with the student using approved materials for exam revision. Disruption to accepted ways of doing things is caused by others and not themselves. Parents and students are the ones who cause conflict and go against accepted norms expected by teachers. The act of disruption or conflict originates elsewhere, away from the teacher who is impacted by such action.

The relatively passive role of the teacher is in their use of syntax, where the cause in the sentence is active and the impact or effect, passive.

Deepa: Yes, so many ... because of nowadays problems ... ladies only ... I'm telling, I'm also lady, problem is from ladies side ... especially I'm telling see ... now rape cases ... so many rape and so many all the dirty things is going on ... because of ladies ... or girls, they don't know how to behave. They are thinking parents have given us freedom some parents won't give.

By frontloading "nowadays problems" with "ladies only", Deepa attributes female rape in India to inappropriate behaviour and parental freedom. "The problem is from the ladies' side", the cause precedes the effect: "so many rape and so many all dirty things" puts across the cause of a serious, widespread issue within Indian society as one primarily with an identifiable protagonist. Problem identification is one that needs an easily identifiable component, often a singular cause that is focused upon and used to understand a widely complex societal issue. This is an oversimplification of a complex issue through an easily understood, accessible cause. It could also be a need to maintain some sense of balance or loyalty to community or societal attitudes. Deepa states that she is also a lady when referring to ladies' misbehaviour, implying that she is aware that her statement is unjust, but within cultural and societal expectations of female behaviour and, being a woman herself, her statement follows accepted cultural attitudes and behaviour. Deepa accepts a passive role in reiterating such narratives, contributing to a disruptive and conflict-ridden narrative itself regarding rape culture within India. This is implicit action, one in which Deepa reiterates and reproduces structural hierarchies and dominant systems (Sugarman and Martin, 2011) within their descriptions of conflict and causes of conflict.

The basis of a meaningful life for teachers

If, as outlined, the protagonists of conflict are those who break relationships, upset balance and whose action is destructive, the purpose of the teacher is founded on their need to maintain relationships, avoid conflict and perform action that is constructive rather than destructive. Teachers' descriptions of their role as educators defined their action as one that helped to build or mould students. This was a central tenet to student interaction and how they saw themselves. In contrast to those they viewed as causing disruption, teachers actively avoided conflict. Non-specific references to other schools or institutions were made along with defensive positioning of their opinions as separate from a wider community or group they represented. Teacher avoidance of conflict could go beyond needing to maintain social relationships to actively demonstrate their core value of building, constructing, and helping to bring students up.

Researcher:	What do you like about teaching?
Amu:	Mainly like the children to get the knowledge and the other things are not throughout the life, but this knowledge what we give, it makes them to stand. We are the pillars so they can stand erect on that, so I love the best to do the children who are not doing it well.
Bhargavi:	Everything is related to the lesson … sometimes when you are taking moral kinds, they have some examples, so what I think … maximum whatever I feel in my heart, I try to just tell the students … I try to make them understand … 'See this is the way, this is the life, society is …' today what we are facing, how we have to be … so by this way, I try to say something.
Celina:	It was cooperative from their side and I used to teach them and bring them to the right path. That was my case.
Deepa:	[B]ut teacher and students means they will bring the children … they will look at like as a mummy or daddy … because of half of the life they spend with us so whatever we say, this is the right way to bring up in their life.

Figure 3.4: Division of internal and external social spaces in relation to external conflict and teachers' productive internal space with their students

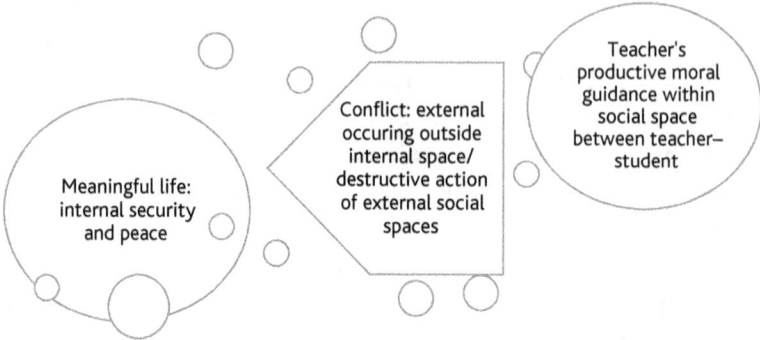

Teachers act as pillars so that students can stand upon them, exhibit freedom to share personal values with students, bringing them onto a 'right path', and act as surrogate parents who advise and guide. The need to be constructive in their relationships with students is a key component of their social interaction, with active teaching of moral education and values within the classroom.

Teachers place themselves as active agents in bringing about such moral guidance, of how to act and live responsibly through being on the right path. Teachers' interpretations of what is right is passed onto the student. Their role as a pillar or their understanding of values and moral guidance are prioritised. Knowledge is built in the student through passing on what the teachers feel is necessary and important for the students. The teachers' moral role is a crucial element of building a relationship with their students, maintaining their positional authority through passing on their values and separating exam performance from moral education and learning. An understanding of meaningful life can be situated within the internal and external social spaces which teachers maintain by avoiding conflict (see Figure 3.4).

Dichotomy of the English language as a space for agency

Peaceful internal and external social spaces are built upon through the role played by the English language, as shown by the interview responses. An interesting discrepancy was revealed between the authority teachers placed on students' use of English, and their own manipulation of the language and its rules to put forward their views.

Amu outlined that having a good command of English enabled students to perform better in school and offered international prospects.

Researcher:	So when they take down from you, they go home and … ?
Amu:	They have to learn … we give them lot of exercises … reading … not only questions and answers … I make them to read the lesson … I want them … first of all, they have to read properly, pronounce the words, understand the meaning of that word … all this is …
Researcher:	Is English very important for this?
Amu:	English is very important, without English they won't know any of the subjects, except the language of Kannada and Hindi … the foremost subject … everything is in English.
Researcher:	Is English important just for their education or for … ?
Amu:	For their life … see when … in my house even to my two daughters we speak only in English because that helps her in her school. What their teacher explains, it will be easy to understand. Their teachers also didn't face much problem, that is what they called and told … the first day my nursery daughter was speaking … communicating in English, so they were very happy.
Researcher:	Why is English so important after you finish school in Bangalore or in India?
Amu:	Anywhere you see, English is the main language, they consider it as an international language, not only anywhere you can go you can survive with that. Job … everything with communication or anything we read from around the globe, if you know English you can survive anywhere.
Researcher:	In particular for their lesson, your students have to know what those words mean?
Amu:	Yes, meanings they should know … even though, I am a science teacher, the English I concentrate … the meaning I want them to understand, without the meaning … formation of sentences

> I can't do. Grammatically even the sentence should be proper ... otherwise no meaning in Science or Social Studies.

Proficiency in English enables communication and global navigation and acts as a survival tool. English is a necessity, not just an ideal or distant objective. As English language is a core skill, students are expected to adhere to the technical aspects of the language, the correct use of grammar, sentence structure and meanings of words. English is a separate, external authority that directs student understanding of all their subjects ("Grammatically even the sentence should be proper ... otherwise no meaning in Science or Social Studies").

Amu's pride in her children being praised for speaking English at primary school level is the beginning of opportunity. The need to learn English extends beyond the demands of a school education to ensuring one's own children's future. Bhargavi's reasons for moving away from the outskirts of the city were motivated by the need to find an English-medium school that provided an English language-based education.

Bhargavi: [I]n Peenya most of the schools are English medium only ... for namesake English-medium school ... almost all the conversation, whatever instructions they are giving, everything is in Kannada only. Students also in Kannada they understand, almost all the conversations are carried out in Kannada only in that school ... Simply, going and saying 'I'm going to an English-medium school' ... knowing about English word[s] means ... so what I thought, I was not interested in the [Kannada-speaking school] area to put my children ...

According to Bhargavi, there is a distinction between schools that tap into a demand for English but supplement teaching in the local language and schools that provide genuine English language education. As with the teacher–student relationship, Bhargavi describes education in schools that teach English through Kannada as one of performance, empty statements to improve their status ("Simply, going and saying 'I'm going to an English-medium school' ... knowing about English word[s] means ..."). The insistence on learning English without the assistance of Kannada to teach or learn it maintains the integrity of English language. Amu and Bhargavi reveal that English as a core skill requires correct understanding and application. English language not only enables further understanding of one's textbooks in school and access to the world but is a language whose authority is to be respected and followed appropriately.

Teachers' use of English language as underlying values of representation

As English language is perceived as immutable, with rigid rules concerning grammar and meanings of words, it would be expected that teachers in interviews would conform to those rules in their own speech. However, what was observed was how the English language was restructured to frame their responses and opinions.

To distinguish their views as individual and not representative of a group, teachers used assertive positioning by using phrases such as 'in my opinion', 'actually' and 'according to me'. They also used defensive positioning with phrases such as 'I am not saying that' or 'not like that' to defend against being misinterpreted or to recall a point previously stated.

Bhargavi:	[I]n my opinion, whatever we teach, we have to teach the children, they have to learn something from us, there has to be a value for education.
Deepa:	Yes, this is as I'm telling myself, I'm not saying others ... why I'm telling others is that I cannot students as example.
Deepa:	I am not saying it was better ... self-satisfaction I am getting it here.
Amu:	Not exactly I don't know about others ... when I see that I focus on that child.

Assertive and defensive positioning allowed teachers to isolate their own opinion from an imagined group or community they may represent within their individual interview. By underlining that it is their opinion, they are aware of their representative role, but also that speaking on their own without group consensus leaves them open and vulnerable to misinterpretation. Amu's use of non-specific references by stating "I don't know about others" refers to other generic schools, but refuses to name them or reveal specific information about teaching practices there.

Figure 3.5: Space for agency to occur between internal language (Kannada) and external form of communication (English language)

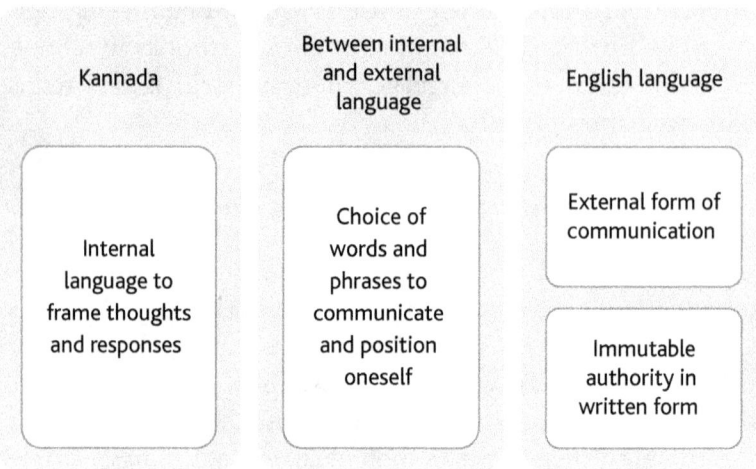

Teachers' use of non-specific descriptors shows a careful choice of words and phrases that allude to a subject or topic while remaining vague and safe. This manoeuvring of language is found in teachers' integrating the English language syntax of subject–verb–object with the local Kannada subject–object–verb as noted in Deepa's response above ("I am not saying it was better ... self-satisfaction I am getting it here"). The integrity of English language syntax is maintained but combined with Kannada. Navigating between two languages demonstrates teachers negotiating between the need to follow the authority of the external language they are communicating in (English) but in conjunction with their internal language which they may be either thinking in or framing their thoughts and responses from. This careful navigation between internal and external language recontextualises the English language as one whose processes and phrases are used to communicate individual responses effectively. The immutable authority of written English language is made malleable when spoken and in response to someone (see Figure 3.5).

Written English is a separate authority whose correct use indicates appropriate education and ability to navigate the world. Teachers' spoken English in interviews is directed by their need to separate their opinion from speaking for others. English provides different functions for teachers and students. Student respect and follow written English language rules, whereas teachers amend and adapt syntax as individual language manipulation.

Teachers were interviewed by an English-speaking researcher using the English language as their main medium of communication. If teachers used their primary language to respond to questions, they may not have produced data in which a distinctive linguistic negotiation took place between the 'subject–object–verb' of Kannada and 'subject–verb–object' of the English language ("That disappointment it is there, today also when I take the class, that time also I'll feel disappointed." [Celina]).

It is the back and forth between the two different syntaxes that brought attention to the way teachers spoke as illuminating. The development context (Sugarman and Martin, 2011) of myself as English-speaking researcher meant that teachers had to negotiate an additional area of communicating in another language while still making meaning. Teachers had to use words that are external to their primary language or internal dialogue. In this act of translation teachers exercised a degree of choice over which words were most appropriate to communicate to myself. Teachers – by moving between one language to another, from one set of words to another set of related words in another language – could be said to have a variable degree of freedom in structuring their speech and choosing words to connect and make meaning.

In order to know or write English, students must follow written grammatical rules. But when it used to speak and answer someone and outline internal thoughts to an external person who only understands through English, those rules are made malleable. Written English rules do not carry through into the communication space, as English is used to communicate and frame your position. This move between the need to frame an internal opinion to external person using a second language that is external, that jumps between internal and external, shows that teachers were active in choosing how they appear to someone in their representation. It is that space between internal thoughts and external phrasing of it to someone that is highly important in understanding teacher's active agency.

Defining teachers' internal and external social spaces

Assertive and defensive positioning is a means of linguistic negotiation where teachers used phrases to distinguish their views as separate from a group they may represent. In addition, teachers avoided specifying places or groups by including a verbal parenthesis that acted as an aside to the main content of their speech.

In discussing students who have picked up bad habits, Deepa used verbal parenthesis followed by non-specific references to distance her students from being included in this group:

Researcher: Do you sometimes see those students?
Deepa: Yeah, many children I have seen ... not our children ... other children I have seen ... especially I am telling in this area, Lingarajapuram.

Adjusting her speech to include the verbal parenthesis of "not our children, other children I have seen", Deepa protects against misrepresenting her students, referring to children in the local area instead. Lingarajapuram becomes the focal point of the sentence and is distanced from Deepa, who had previously stated that she was not from the area and preferred other parts of Bangalore. The verbal parenthesis acts as a corrective device, to steer the sentence towards being non-specific and to a generic local area. Deepa not only protected her students and her school but also articulated her awareness of how she may be interpreted.

Bhargavi used non-specific references to use describe how she disciplines her students:

Bhargavi: [O]therwise ... we say it once or twice ... 'in case if you don't obey, I'll give you punishment' we'll say ... by giving something imposition, that you'll not do certain things, you'll write certain times ... saying like this ... sometimes, I'll say 'Write, I'll not talk in class' ... more than that we don't give.

In ending the sentence with "more than that we don't give", Bhargavi avoided being specific about what she meant by further punishment. While being specific about addressing her students with verbal warnings, Bhargavi alluded to further punishment, specifying that they do not do it. The use of a non-specific reference in "more than that" followed by a specific "we don't give", demonstrates that Bhargavi was aware of what not to say or to allude to instead of being specific. Whether "more than that" indicates physical punishment or something harsher than verbal warnings, being specific about it indicates knowledge of such punishment. Mentioning these in a discussion of student discipline would not only give the researcher the wrong impression of the teacher and the school but may detract from previous statements made.

Bhargavi and Deepa were not only self-aware, but their heightened self-awareness gives us a glimpse of how they navigate between themselves, their communities, or the groups they represented. Verbal parentheses and non-specific references allow us to see how negotiation takes place, guarding against misrepresentation, being protective and communal but also purposefully corrective by either avoiding or misdirecting attention to something non-specific and generic. This indicates a clear and distinct skill in linguistic manipulation of spoken syntax: to put across a point, to put forward a representation but also to guard against misinterpretation and facilitate deflection.

Amu uses defensive positioning and non-specific references to focus attention on her action with the student:

Researcher:	Do you think that some of them don't get that opportunity to have that?
Amu:	Not exactly I don't know about others … when I see that I focus on that child, those who don't do anything, they are very weak.

In responding to a question on opportunities to develop knowledge and wisdom among students, Amu redirects her response away from discussing external factors that contribute to student knowledge to what she does to help students. This form of circumvention protects oneself from commenting on factors outside the classroom and redirecting discussion to their individual action. Amu takes control of our conversation, redirecting a question to respond in the way she chooses to. By avoiding talking about others and refocusing on herself, we now focus on her teaching techniques and problem-solving skills. This helps understand how teachers use phrases to not only reconstruct speech but to refocus attention on their action or opinion. Moving my focus away from the whole, from the community or group they represent to themselves, demonstrates an ability to separate themselves from the group itself. The underlying motivation to separate oneself is still defined by the needs of the group, to protect community representation to the outsider-researcher.

In terms of representation(Spivak, 2005), teachers' use of language reveals not just a need to protect a collective against misrepresentation but a skilled use of speech to redirect focus and attention for a particular purpose. It is the act of bringing my attention in line with the view or perspective they wish to put across that is most interesting. There is a certain amount of control when explicating statements or clarifying phrases. Despite teachers' apparent hesitance or use of fragmented non-specific phrases, avoidance indicates a distinctive understanding and control of their representation through language. The teacher may sound flustered or backtrack using broken phrases, but there is a certain clarity of purpose and skill between how they sound to myself and what they want to get across. This is not just simple purposeful obfuscation but part of their spoken syntax, the nature of their speech, to backtrack, to reiterate, to be non-specific. However, in the free-flowing, fluid nature of spoken speech, it does highlight a certain level of control in deflecting focus away from a previous statement and redirecting towards their intended meaning.

The way teachers respond in their speech to others, helps define their relationships with others, and brings to the surface relationships and social constructs in which they are embedded. How teachers perceive the relationship between themselves and myself, and between themselves, is demonstrated through how they speak. Reconstructing one's speech enables teachers to define relationships and helps them navigate their social spaces, demarcating views or opinions that need protection from outside intrusion and those that are shared externally.

Speech, space and relational agency

A conscious act of agency, in the form of intentional individual action, may not be possible where roles and relationships are embedded, and where the dynamics of relationships are implicit and not articulated. It is difficult to put forward an act of agency if your role and those you are directing it to are embedded. Power dynamics and structural hierarchies are not defined as such but part of your everyday existence and routine. However, it is possible to view acts of agency in the way one speaks and how social actors frame agency through their careful navigation of their social spaces through how they speak to others.

Agency is, therefore, in a continual state of negotiation and renegotiation, in which the teacher consistently adjusts and readjusts their choice of words and structure of speech to communicate and relate to their listener. In this sense, agency is fluid, dynamic and based on communication, making it fundamentally relational. As with Burkitt's understanding of relational agency as based in interaction and interdependence (Burkitt, 2016), teachers adjust their speech to external perceptions, to someone or something they are mutually dependent on within their conversation. Teachers' use of language can have crucial consequences for an understanding of agency defined by its relationship to others, as relational agency (Gergen, 2011; Sugarman and Martin, 2011). Within an equal relationship between people, one can exert one's voice to contest something within the relationship or conform to it (loyalty). One can also leave the relationship (exit) and end it (De Herdt and Bastiaensen, 2008). Within unequal, asymmetrical relationships, the choice to leave and exit is removed, leaving loyalty as the main function of the relationship, as contest through voice is disenabled. A lack of voice (De Herdt and Bastiaensen, 2008) indicates marginalised status.

Teachers' speech is a form of agency that takes place within an interdependent context in which teacher and researcher are bound in narrative dialogue. Verbal speech, as opposed to written speech is more fluid, iterative and to some extent unstructured. The unstructured nature of conversation between myself and the teacher allowed them to reconstruct points they were making while speaking. They could go back and reposition, reiterate, and clarify. This enabled a space in which they could exercise a form of agency. It is the nature of speech – the way teachers use language –and not just the content of what is said that is an act of agency.

Literature concerning voice and relational agency (De Herdt and Bastiaensen, 2008; Clegg, 2011; Gergen, 2011; Sugarman and Martin, 2011) has emphasised the content of what is said by people. Agential action through speaking up, through using one's voice to conform or contest, is prioritised over the nature of speech itself. I believe that spoken speech can contribute to a richer understanding of relational agency that includes the nature of how one speaks and not just what they say. This is especially useful in examining agency for those who reproduce dominant systems and structures (Sugarman and Martin, 2011; Burkitt, 2016). Looking at the way they speak, the nature of their speech can have crucial implications for a more distinct understanding of relational agency within these groups.

Voice as agency for the female teacher

The teacher's voice is dominant within the classroom, establishing their authority when they speak and commanding reciprocal silence by students. Voice as agentive freedom is made possible in the positional authority the teacher has with their students, something that is presupposed within the Indian teacher–student relationship. Teachers can exercise agency within the classroom, yet such agency is still managed through gender-oriented roles between female teacher and student. As discussed previously, the maternal role of the teacher underlines the nature of care between a teacher and a student, utilising a dominant and accepted gendered relation in which the maternal teacher is allowed to scold and encourage as a mother would her child (Gupta, 2003). The mother's voice is central to this dynamic. Therefore, a teacher's voice helps to fulfil their ability to discipline and control this relationship. If this ability to use their voice is taken away, it contributes to a sense of futility as Deepa points out:

Deepa: [S]o I feel here if we scold the children, we say some good things, parent used to come 'Why did you say like that to my child?', here I feel somewhat ... nothing useful to say ... no future for children also for teacher also, I feel ...

The female teacher can facilitate agency through voice by using accepted gender relations to encourage and scold within the classroom. Here, she can withdraw from dialogue with the student, contest responses and express loyalty if she chooses ("nothing useful to say"). However, teacher's agency is underwritten by a maternal role and, although it enables and supports her positional authority within the classroom, it can also limit action to her role as teacher and the place in which this occurs, the classroom.

Agency as founded on interaction and social connections (Burkitt, 2016) is significant in understanding a female teacher's agency. She uses her voice to interact with her students, enabled by an embedded maternal, gendered relationship in which she can exercise a degree of agentive freedom to contest, exit and conform (de Herdt and Bastiaensen, 2008).

If agency is defined through interaction with others, the act of constructing and reconstructing responses can act to self-evaluate one's responses in relation to questions. This concurs with Gergen's (Gergen, 2011) avocation of the relational being, who continues relation with others when describing themselves. This is reflected in the way teachers describe their roles as women and as teachers, the way they teach or their understanding of learning and knowledge as based on a foundation of relationships, of who they are to others and what they do. If a core element of a low-income female teacher's experience is to adjust, reconstruct and reorganise, whether it is in terms of speech or in meeting professional and personal expectations, teachers are in constant engagement with their environment and their role within it.

Relational agency can help inform how teachers evaluate themselves in relation to contexts in which they are interlinked and interdependent. Freedom of choice underlined by an individual's journey of self-knowledge and grounded in individual agency (Giddens, 1991) can instead be viewed, among the teachers interviewed, as an understanding of a self-guided by relational agency that maintains mutual dependencies and interdependent relationships.

Linguistic negotiation of speech as acts of agency relates to Spivak's (Spivak, 2005) unrepresented female subaltern. Spivak states representation through collective identity can help avoid a politics of recognition in which there is a conflict in terms of who recognises the subaltern's representation and how it is to be received. Teachers' agency through their speech is a means of representation, of putting forward what they want to say and to whom, as a collective group of low-income female teachers. Teachers did collectively identify as teachers in interviews and group discussions. The embedded and entangled nature of their collective identity, as low-income female teachers, meant that representation was not necessarily through direct self-identification or examination. It was through their careful navigation of social spaces mediated by their speech. Teachers who were interviewed individually agreed with their peers in a group setting and attempted to speak with a collective voice.

Considering the idiographic research focus on the individual perspectives of teachers, the need to provide a collective representation by the teachers interviewed made highlighting individual views problematic. This did help bring teachers together, but it did not help avoid a politics of recognition: teachers were acutely aware of who recognises their collective representation and how it should be perceived by outsiders. The complexities of representation for teachers are further understood through their speech. Spivak's 'synecdoche' may provide a form of self-representation but, within this research context, it does so as a collective, making individual representation problematic. In relation to teachers' responses, individual and collective identity are subsumed. This has brought difficulties in examining the individual views and opinions of teachers, especially given my research focus on individual perspectives.

Implications for reflective practice in teacher education

If agency is defined through interaction with others, constructing and reconstructing responses can act as a form of self-evaluation. This concurs with Gergen's (Gergen, 2011) avocation of the relational being, who defines themselves through descriptions of their relationships with others. This is reflected in the way teachers describe their roles as women, as teachers, as the way they teach or who they are to others and what they do. If a core element of a low-income female teacher's experience is to adjust, reconstruct and reorganise, whether it is in their speech or in meeting professional and personal obligations, teachers are in constant engagement with their environment and their role within it.

Relational agency can help inform how teachers evaluate themselves in relation to contexts in which they are interlinked and interdependent. Freedom of choice underlined by an individual's journey of self-knowledge and grounded in individual agency (Giddens, 1991) can instead be viewed, among the teachers interviewed, as an understanding of a self, guided by relational agency that maintains mutual dependencies and interdependent relationships.

Linguistic negotiation of speech as acts of agency relates to Spivak's (Spivak, 2005) unrepresented female subaltern. Spivak states representation through collective identity can help avoid a politics of recognition in which there is a conflict between who recognises the subaltern's representation and how it is to be received. Teachers' agency through their speech is a means of representation, of putting forward what they want to say and to whom as a collective group of low-income female teachers. Teachers did collectively identify as teachers in interviews and group discussions. The embedded and entangled nature of their collective identity, as low-income female teachers, meant that representation was not necessarily through their direct self-identification or examination. It was through their careful navigation of social spaces mediated by their speech. Teachers who were interviewed individually agreed with their peers in a group setting and attempted to speak with a collective voice.

Considering the research focus on individual perspectives of teachers, the need to provide a collective representation by teachers interviewed meant that highlighting individual views became problematic. A politics of recognition could not be avoided as teachers were acutely aware of who recognises their collective representation and how it should be perceived by outsiders. Spivak's 'synecdoche' may provide a form of self-representation, but within teachers' responses, representation is through a collective, making individual representation problematic. Individual and collective identities are subsumed within representation and impact the ability for individual teachers to self-evaluate and reflect on their practice without their implicit navigation between their internal and external social spaces.

The protagonists of conflict are often external to the teacher, whether they be student, parent or society in general. Conflict occurs 'out there' and not necessarily 'in here', within one's internal space whether that be private, individual, or collective. Values defined by internal-external social spaces avoid examining the internal, 'in here' space. This is actualised in teachers' speech to defend themselves and attribute the cause of problems as external to themselves. The ability to take ownership of one's failure, or individual act of discord or disagreement, is hindered by placing protagonists of conflict as those outside who threaten collective and communal accord. This significantly impacts the ability of the individual to take responsibility for their actions and to identify problems within their own teaching practice. The inability to look within and own one's mistakes, or identify areas that need to be improved, is supported by the need to preserve one's internal space from those who create destruction and disunity.

Therefore, issues with developing self-evaluation and critical reflection within training programmes centre upon conflict avoidance exhibited by teachers. Training may need to consider underlying issues with problem identification as external to the teacher that prevents internal reflection or questioning. Taking apart oneself and one's attitudes to analyse relationships and critically reflect on these may not be compatible within this context. However, emphasising the nature of speech in how individuals speak and evaluating how they come across could help develop initial understanding of deconstruction and problem identification.

Training that enables teachers to identify processes of their speech, how they describe their duties, roles, responsibilities, and words to describe students and expectations can help form the basis for

Table 3.3: Teachers' perspectives on navigating social spaces in relation to reflective practice

Teacher's perspectives on navigating social spaces: *Mediating internal and external social spaces through speech*	Agentive action through process of speech	Implications for reflective practice in teacher education in India
	Teachers' act of agency emerges through navigating between social spaces as they choose words/phrases to define how they will be perceived and represented to an outsider	*Examining conflict avoidance as key to problem identification* Training can approach problem idenfication through a deeper understanding of conflict avoidance and the need for self-preservation
	Conflict is external and occurs outside one's internal space	
	Protagonists are parents, those in authority who criticise teachers. External action is destructive whilst teacher action is constructive and maintains social cohesion in internal spaces.	Training can focus on descriptions of conflict and perceived protagonists of conflict to enable teachers to examine their understanding of failure and ownership of individual errors

later stages of taking these apart: moving toward questioning but considering the dynamics of conflict avoidance, self-preservation, and gendered space that these teachers inhabit.

Training can initiate problem identification by emphasising how conflict is described and who or what are protagonists of perceived conflict (see Table 3.3). Training programmes that examine teachers' speech in attributing blame or culpability for discord can enable teachers to approach their own individual acts of conflict and discord and ownership of mistakes and problems. This might not be sufficient to address individual and personal underlying sources of conflict avoidance, but it could enable a technical focus on speech and social relations within one's teaching practice as part of professional development.

4

Teachers' attitudes to transformation

This chapter outlines the role knowledge plays in achievement, social emancipation and transformation (see Figure 4.1). Teacher's positional authority is examined in order to understand female empowerment and agency. Fundamental to this is the teacher's voice as the main instrument of knowledge distribution and agency within the classroom. The nature of authentic knowledge as defining teacher's attitudes to transformation is be examined. First, my role within this research is outlined so as to provide a background of critical researcher reflexivity that can help introduce teacher attitudes to transformation for themselves and their students (see Table 4.1). My need to maintain objective distance yet also acknowledge the impact of my position and privilege when meeting with and conversing with teachers acts as a valuable foundation to examine statements made by teachers on their predominance in their students' achievement and transformation. Implications of these attitudes for reflective practice in teacher education conclude this chapter.

Critical researcher reflexivity

A key basis of this chapter is the impact of the methodological considerations of my research in defining how data was collected and subsequent analysis and theory developed. The processes by which validity was maintained during data collection and analysis reflect the discussion within this chapter of what constitutes authentic knowledge

Figure 4.1: Chapter 4 outline

Table 4.1: Teachers' attitudes to transformation in relation to reflective practice

Teachers' attitudes to transformation: *Authentic knowledge and distributed personhood of knowledge. Moral educator role and understanding of transformation.*	Authentic knowledge and distributed personhood of knowledge	Implications for reflective practice in teacher education in India
	Authentic, authoritative knowledge is based on personhood, who provides knowledge and where it comes from rather than knowledge derived from empirical observation and critical self-reflexive analysis	Training can examine what teachers define as knowledge and how knowledge is producted
	Use of description, narratives and examples and use of statives
Limits further explanation or developing inquiry within the classroom and in teachers' descriptions of their role	Training can explore teacher understanding and expectations of classroom dialogue and discursive practice. Training can focus on adapting teacher's spoken syntax to enable student interpretation and analysis of textbook material.
	Teacher as builder
Teaching as constructive action that builds values, relationships and knowledge tranformation as including moral education along with academic achievement as part of teacher's duty towards their students	Training can consider a teacher's moral educator role and understanding of transformation. A focus on words and verbal interaction with students can help teachers explore transformative, constructive acts of teaching from a foundational teaching technique, their speech.

and transformation for teachers and students. I had taken steps to acknowledge the presence and impact of myself as researcher on the nature of data I collected and analysed. In the same vein, my efforts to ensure content validity —acknowledging and attempting to restrict my position of power as a researcher— provides an ideological foil to core issues within this chapter, where teachers' ideas of transformation vary considerably and include that which is distributed, disseminated and demonstrative of their authority and impact on the student.

I employed critical researcher reflexivity throughout data collection and analysis so that I could consider my own position in relation to teachers, especially my need to provide them with a platform to demonstrate agency and voice. It was important to consider power relationships between myself and teachers, given our different socio-economic backgrounds and my 'outsider' status (Robinson-Pant and Singal, 2013a, 2013b). To counteract imposing my views and need to speak for teachers, data findings and analysis attempted to avoid definitive statements of teacher behaviour, instead emphasising my interpretation of data. This is particularly significant for content validity (Cohen, Manion and Morrison, 2007) in which abstract notions or ideas as interpreted by the researcher are generally accepted.

In this case, my understanding of agency and use of spoken syntax by teachers defines my analysis of their speech, along with theories of relational agency. I have attempted to let teachers guide my data analysis, yet I still needed to employ preliminary theoretical constructs to define codes (Malterud, 2001; Cohen, Manion and Morrison, 2007; Hammersley, 2007). Thus, I encountered a distinct space between intending to give primacy to each teacher's voice and yet needing to understand it through accepted theory and literature.

In addition, by focusing on speech patterns I attempted to regulate over-interpretation through a systematic method to examine and analyse data through syntax codes. Systematic syntax codes examined teacher speech, rich in data and detail, using a method that provided a degree of rigour by stepping back and approaching what teachers said through how they spoke. Creswell and Miller (Creswell and Miller, 2000) align themselves with systematic paradigms that acknowledge reflexive practice to develop credibility within qualitative research. Hammersley (Hammersley, 2007), advocates methodological pluralism to guide research and the benefits of assessment criteria within qualitative research. Criteria can provide the space to reflect upon interpretive judgements and examine their applicability within different contexts.

In relation to this research, criteria outlined that spoken syntax and speech is limited to low-income female teachers in Bangalore and does not seek to analyse other socio-economic or gender groups within India or elsewhere. However, as Hammersley points out, the process of applying criteria to different contexts could develop research practice through reflection for the researcher. Applying spoken syntax to teacher education within India requires consistent reflection by myself regarding my role within research analysis, the relevance of my analysis to research questions, and the applicability of such analysis to a different teacher education context. Data analysis requires multiple stages in which checks and balances are employed to improve the credibility of data and practical applicability. Using systematic methods such as discourse analysis tools of inquiry to examine spoken syntax enabled an analysis of teachers' speech in relation to wider values held as a group, while still giving primacy to the individual voice and story of the teacher within analysis.

It is important to note the colonial underpinnings of ethnographic research among marginalised groups in India when conducting research. The development of ethnography away from previous restrictive paradigms does not guard against contemporary dilemmas when researching in postcolonial contexts (Fox, 2008). I needed to consider the impact of self-exploratory and reflective research for women who may not have recounted their life history before or made connections to their attitudes towards capability for themselves and their students (Rizvi et al, 2006; Robinson-Pant and Singal, 2013b). I designed interview questions to allow for open-ended responses, avoiding direct questions that prompted specific reflection or questions that framed a judgement or researcher bias. I sought teachers' views and opinions within my initial questions, with additional questions based on their responses. It was important that, as I conversed with individual teachers, I allowed myself to engage naturally with their responses; this included emotional investment in their stories and appropriate conciliatory responses if needed. In group discussions, scenarios with generic examples were used to avoid using examples from individual teachers' descriptions to maintain their confidentiality.

As mentioned, a key method employed to support validity was a commitment to critical research reflexivity. This meant that I needed continually to reflect and evaluate how I collected data and how this impacted analysis and theory generated from data. It is this process of self-evaluation leading towards change that underpins this chapter's focus on how teachers view transformation for themselves and their students. Habermas is significant in outlining a view of authentic knowledge and social praxis that can help us understand how teachers defined their own understanding of this within their teaching practice.

Authentic knowledge and social praxis within teachers' responses

Reflective practice incorporates key elements related to the ability to reflect upon past experiences, events and action to learn from experiences and be prepared for similar experiences that would occur in the future (Dewey, 2011). Reflecting upon the past can extend beyond functionalist preparation for the future and into developing unique, individual perspectives on your actions and experiences to consider your motivations related to those experiences. Reflective practice can consider the foundations of past action within contexts that may cover individual, social and cultural contexts. Cunliffe (Cunliffe, 2009) outlines self-reflexivity as based upon how an individual questions their assumptions, values and relationships with others as they shape and are shaped by social experiences. This self-dialogue leads to more responsive and positive means of communication with others. Critical self-reflexivity considers one's assumptions within a wider context of society, multiplicity of views and impact of social assumptions on groups and sections of society. Individual assumptions are placed within a larger context and viewed through a comprehensive, critical frame instigating reflection on one's views and actions as contributing to social relationships at a broader societal level.

For teachers, self-reflexive and critical self-reflexivity is fundamental to a teacher's ability to assess their assumptions and values in relation to their role, learning and to their students. Power structures within a teacher–student relationship, as well as assumptions about student learning and ability, greatly impact the relationship between teacher and student, which in turn impacts student learning.

Habermas (Lovat, 2013) viewed reflection in terms of self-knowing. This was a key stage of higher thinking and whose forward direction is towards effective social action. Habermas's stages of knowledge development begin with empirical knowledge as acquiring all forms of knowledge to instigate hermeneutic connections in which categories of knowledge are linked and develop self-knowing. Here, the connections one makes, and their meaning, become one's own authentic knowledge. As with Freire (1996), self-knowing insists upon confronting one's past, beliefs and values in both personal and social spheres. Crucially, development of critical self-knowing enables one to let go of the past and embrace new futures.

Indian literature highlights historical and cultural references as well as teachers' emancipation from restrictive structures. With Habermas, authentic knowledge could allow teachers to make sense of the connections they make in their daily lives. Authentic knowledge allows for reflections that may be fluid and reciprocal in relation to family and social obligations. It could reiterate and reproduce collective/hierarchical notions of knowledge and behaviourist approaches.

Habermas situates education's role within a critical self-reflexive stage. The consequence or product of critical self-knowing is praxis, towards a practical application of knowledge for change (see Figure 4.2). As knowing is crucial to value formation, social and moral responsibilities are essentially educational. Therefore, teacher's praxis is effective social action in the way they encourage hermeneutic communication from their students to facilitate authentic, self-knowing. The way that teachers practically apply their authentic knowledge for change in their students is to support students towards their own authentic knowledge developed from making connections.

Praxis is aligned with symmetrical relationships between teacher and student, enabling a reversal of roles where the teacher becomes a learner. It is within praxis based on committed, altruistic action that a developed form of thinking, a higher stage of moral development and critical reasoning is most effective. For this, a teacher's values are central. Reflective practice, how we learn from experience is a process through which we encounter and engage with our values and whose praxis is a forward action to inform not only our professional practice but our social action and transformation.

Given the strong asymmetrical relationship between the Indian teacher and student, this aspect of critical self-reflection may be distinctly problematic. However, the nature of the relationship between teacher and student where the teacher's emotional investment takes on a maternal role (Gupta, 2003; Joshi, 2009) indicates that teachers' commitment to their students is not restricted to stringent power relations but is one that references how care is reinforced by social and cultural value systems (see Figure 4.3). Teachers' commitment to their student through a socially accepted maternal role can help form a foundation for social action. This ties in with notions of the ascetic ideal as well as building upon teachers' investment in the achievements of their students and their role and contribution to their students' transformation. At the heart of this is teachers' understanding of what a student is capable of and the importance of academic achievement for future success that feeds into their social praxis and social action.

Academic achievement for future success

Teachers did, in general, concur with literature on student aspirations, expectations of achievement and student behaviour in the importance

Teachers' attitudes to transformation

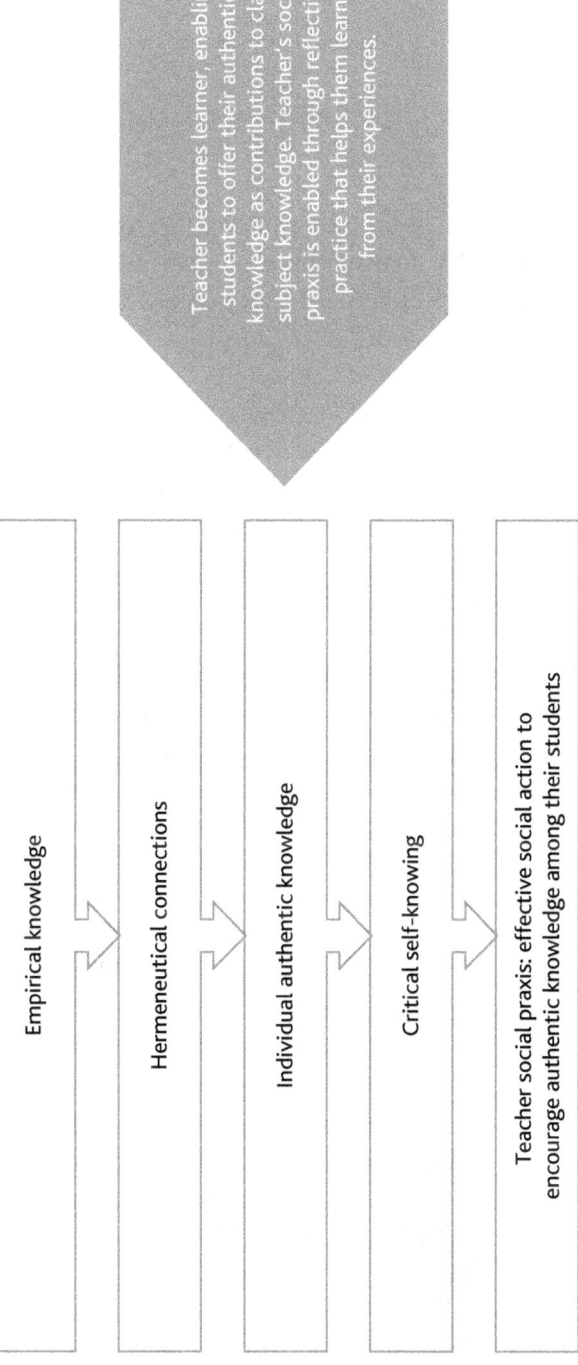

Figure 4.2: Habermas's development of authentic knowledge and social praxis

Source: Based on Lovat, 2013

Figure 4.3: Low-income female teachers' social praxis as defined by responses

Low-income female teacher's social praxis ⇒ Maternal role of care as social action: emotional investment in student achievement ⇒ Socially accepted gendered position that maintains assymetrical relationships

of academic achievement for future success (Sarangapani, 2003; Mooij, 2008; Morrow, 2013; Ganapathy-Coleman, 2014). Amu outlined that those higher marks led to a greater choice in colleges leading to a higher level of profession.

Amu: Accordingly to the parents' wish and to their ambition, almost they have chosen that. But sometimes some child will want to do medicine, engineering so some of them are not able to achieve that ... because of the rankings went down ... sometimes they want to do big management quotas ... huge amount, sometimes they were not able to pay that ... so they went for a lower degree ... not lower degree they went for a normal degree, BSc or ...

Researcher: So do they have to compromise with their parents? Get their permission?

Amu: Even parents are worried, if they would have achieved within their marks, scorings, even with the less amount they would've joined.

Researcher: So there is a lot of pressure for them to get good marks, standards?

Amu: Ah, yes, it is there because when they take science stream, so that time they have the time CET [Common Entrance] exams, the rankings are there. If they have a good ranking, definitely they will achieve that. Sometimes they are lagging in that.

Researcher: So the higher the marks they have ...

Amu: The more choice they have.

Amu specifically referred to higher marks as increasing choice: students must work harder at school to have a choice for their future. As indicated in Chapter 2, a hard-working student was one who closely followed the teacher's instructions and accepted their knowledge. Greater control of learning at school can afford greater freedom of choice for their future ("the rankings are there. If they have a good ranking, definitely they will achieve that. Sometimes they are lagging in that."). Rank indicates the sum of a student's academic performance in high school, where the higher the mark and rank, the greater choice in educational, professional and lifestyle choices in the future.

Bhargavi agreed that higher marks were needed but so was talent, in her description of student ambition and achievement after school.

Researcher:	So should this carry on after they finish school? If they have that ambition, 'Miss, I want to become an engineer', when they finish high school … how easy or difficult is it to go ahead and become an engineer?
Bhargavi:	Again what we are saying … again if they are changing for their ideas and mind … so we are helpless, we can't do anything, it is left to their option … we can't interfere … they are free to choose their own choice … we cannot go and force them.
Researcher:	Do they have to have very high marks?
Bhargavi:	Yes … at the same time they should be having talent also.

As with Amu, Bhargavi brings forward the choice available to the student. She agrees that high marks are important, but states talent is needed as well, with no further explanation for what constitutes talent. Here, Bhargavi differs from Amu in their understandings of choice by emphasising talent alongside exam performance. Student achievement is not just restricted to grades but to qualities inherent in the student. Whereas Amu outlined exam performance in securing greater educational opportunities, Bhargavi places its overall significance into context in a way that is echoed by Celina and Deepa.

In a discussion on Celina's desire to prepare university students for exams, she felt a degree certificate mainly helped secure employment for students:

Celina:	Nowadays children are only preparing for the examination, not for the knowledge. They wanted

	to have a degree certificate, for the sake of that they are motivated.
Researcher:	What does that certificate mean for them? Is it a job?
Celina:	It's a job for them ... you don't have a certificate they won't give you a job ... therefore money.

As with Amu, employment is the main objective. However, Celina sees this as a value held by her students, not necessarily by herself, when referring to students preparing for exams and not for knowledge ("They wanted to have a degree certificate, for the sake of that they are motivated"). Celina sees external factors, such as the need for social and economic achievement, that relegate learning and knowledge to serve as functionary of such needs. She outlines the distinction between learning and exam preparation. The latter is separated from obtaining or demonstrating understanding of knowledge and is mainly a means to employment and subsequently money.

The emphasis on money is supported by Deepa when describing the demands of a competitive world and the need for academic achievement or business skills and money to succeed.

Researcher:	When those students leave Standard 10 and go out from school, what do they normally end up doing, do you know?
Deepa:	They will fail, obviously they will fail ... according to me, failing in examination is not a big issue ... we have to face our problems in life, that I used to say to my children, I used to say ... 'You have to pass, get the good marks' ... of course, some children they don't have talent but they will come up in their life in a good way, other way they will come up.
Researcher:	Why is it important to get good marks?
Deepa:	Good marks actually ... now it is a competitive world so to get one good job, so they need marks but if they want to do any business, no need to do any ... any exams, marks, and all.
Researcher:	Why is it for business you don't need marks?
Deepa:	No need ... because we are putting our money, we are investing our money, no need a degree ... according to me study is nothing but we have to improve our knowledge.

Deepa's statement that failing is not an issue yet advising students to get good marks may seem contradictory at first; however, it places into context exam performance within perceived social realities ("now it is a competitive world so to get one good job, so they need marks"). Deepa navigates between putting forward the need for good exam performance as part of her professional duty as a teacher and also getting across her personal views ("according to me study is nothing but we have to improve our knowledge").

Deepa distinguishes between getting good grades to secure a job and the irrelevance of exams to do well in business. Business necessitates self-investment and does not require skills or knowledge obtained through high school exams or learning. Deepa separates being an employee of someone and being self-employed as one where educational achievement and success lead to financial capital for employees, but those self-employed rely on their own money to increase their financial capital. This places those without financial capital as essentially dependent on those that can employ them. It is not necessarily the case that lower-income students are required to study more than higher-income students, but that the consequences of failing to obtain sufficient grades at high school are graver without the backup of financial capital, usually provided by one's family.

This reveals an interesting discrepancy between teachers' statements. Learning operates on two different levels: one in which the student learns from the teacher to obtain good grades and subsequent educational choice and financial capacity; and the other, in which learning is separate, not linked to any further function than for increasing knowledge. Academic achievement for these teachers is exam performance. This is hinted at by Bhargavi and Deepa in their allusion to a student's inherent abilities through talent, but not necessarily as important or crucial as exams in helping to secure the student's educational and financial future success.

Teacher views of their sense of achievement

Teacher relationships with their students were outlined as a marker of their achievement, often because of their hard work and investment in their students and the future gratitude of the student.

With Amu and Bhargavi, the verbal recognition of gratitude by students was important to underline their sense of achievement:

Amu:	In science, they have to do that ... physically they have to but mentally there was lagging behind with their studies and all, so we used to focus a bit more on that. So their efforts were more.
Researcher:	Did they recognise this when they received their marks?
Amu:	They were very happy, it made me also very happy. Later on they realised it, 'It's only because of you, Ma'am, we got this' ... in the end they were very happy.
Researcher:	Do you feel you have got a sense of achievement in all your years as a teacher?
Bhargavi:	Yeah, something ... a good friendship with the students, daily they come running after me, wherever they see me, you know ... they come even if I don't observe them on the way also while going, they call me and stop me and come and speak to me.

Amu and Bhargavi describe their good relationships with students through recalled speech and narrative; student gratitude was not only a marker of teachers' sense of achievement but also demonstrates their ability to engender such gratitude. It is not just the social relationships that indicate a teacher's achievement but the need for demonstrative verbal engagement that underlines such social relation from student to teacher. This concurs with how teachers described the need for students to respond verbally to them. However in this case, the students instigate social relation ("they call me and stop me and come and speak to me" [Bhargavi]). Verbal gratitude is held onto and retold to others such as myself, to indicate their effectiveness as a teacher. The narrative of student gratitude is placed in a wider narrative of teacher achievement.

As with Amu and Bhargavi, Celina and Deepa's sense of achievement is founded in the relationships with their students, however with differences in what they expect from students.

Researcher:	What is the sense of achievement you've felt in your 23 years of teaching?
Celina:	Love and affection to students ... devoting myself to them, without expecting something from them, I'm doing it.

Teachers' attitudes to transformation

Researcher: In your years of teaching, what kind of sense of achievement do you feel you have achieved as a teacher?

Deepa: Yeah, I have improved my knowledge and meanwhile I can understand the children, five fingers are not the same, one child is entirely different, one more child is entirely different. So I can understand and make them how to lead their life. That is mine ... and be happy about this teaching field.

Celina puts across her devotion to students. This is viewed from a particularly maternal perspective but also as a way of distinguishing herself as a teacher for whom achievement is her relationship to her students, without expectations of mutual or reciprocal gratitude or action. By not expecting anything from her students, her motivations are separated from a sense of moral economy or mutuality. Her achievement is one that is pure or removed from student obligation to their teacher, demonstrating that she may be aware of how she is perceived in outlining this, and what kind of image she wants to put across.

Deepa focuses on providing the right kind of moral advice. In contrast to the others, her sense of achievement is within her intellectual engagement in developing her understanding or knowledge about her students. This acts as a foundation to provide moral support and advice and one in which she finds happiness in her profession.

All teachers were distinct in placing their sense of achievement within their relationships with students, whether through demonstrative verbal gratitude, unconditional devotion or developing awareness of students to deliver effective moral advice. Teachers' understanding of student achievement was essentially functional, to secure educational and financial opportunities, whereas their own sense of achievement was grounded in their effectiveness to provide for the student. Although these are differing approaches to the way achievement is understood by teachers, the emphasis on performance, on active demonstration of ability is evident in both approaches to student and teacher achievement. Students are required to perform at summative exams, demonstrating their ability to put into practice teacher instruction, whereas teachers rely on social relation to confirm their performance, either through gratitude, devotional action or moral guidance. Achievement in this sense is relational, as circumscribed by mutual relationships and social interactions between student and teacher.

This has distinct consequences for understanding how aspirations are formed and negotiated when parents and teachers are rigid in their expectations and the student/child malleable. Identifying how to develop and improve oneself is therefore problematic if one has been directed on what to work towards and how to achieve this as well as to share such achievement with those who instructed them.

Bhargavi describes the need for students to recognise the different hardships parents go through to make education possible for their children and the efforts of their school:

Bhargavi: One thing we used to say to them … after you finish, see it will be good for you … don't spoil your school name, reputation as far as you're in the school, we get good name to the school … and to your teachers, your parents also … they are the ones who take so much of difficulty and sending you to school, taking care of each and everything for you, all your needs … how much ever troubles come in their life they are ready to face everything for the sake of children … so don't forget these things … keep in your mind. First of all, think of your parents, ones who have given you all this, you should be very lucky enough to sit, to get such good parents … for providing each and everything in your life … and thankful to the God … don't ever forget the school and teachers who gave you the education so not now, in your future.

The joint effort of parent and teacher in working to help the student/child be successful demands the reciprocal act of acknowledgement and gratitude. This is not strictly an act of moral economy in which a student through gratitude returns the hard work and effort of parents and teachers, but where reciprocal gratitude acknowledges them. It shows respect and reminds the student their individual achievement is due to the work of those before them ("you should be very lucky enough to sit, to get such good parents … for providing each and everything in your life"). The need for reciprocal gratitude also maintains the asymmetrical relationship between parent/teacher and student/child.

Amu builds upon this when describing the achievement of a recent student cohort:

Researcher: Why did they achieve such good marks?
Amu: I feel the students ... they were happy with me ... happiness in the sense, they were not very happy with me, I was very strict ... not cut jokes, laugh with them, always I will be very strict. I keep concentrating on the work only, even sometimes their PT [physical training] period, sometimes I will take because at the end and all, I don't allow them ... but I will say it is very good for playing and all that, I give the instruction. In science, they have to do that ... physically they have to but mentally there was lagging behind with their studies and all, so we used to focus a bit more on that. So their efforts were more.
Researcher: Did they recognise this when they received their marks?
Amu They were very happy, it made me also very happy. Later on they realised it, 'It's only because of you, Ma'am, we got this' ... in the end they were very happy.

Students' acknowledgement of Amu's efforts occurred after they received their marks, as a final credit to their teacher's strict discipline. This feeds into the idea that the student, in the act of learning, is inherently unaware of the reality of hard work, of adult efforts to provide, direct and ensure their success ("Later on they realised it, 'It's only because of you, Ma'am, we got this'"). It also distinguishes the teacher as understanding the world in which they live and the student as outside this sphere of understanding. Amu and Bhargavi outlined student gratitude as confirming their efforts and hard work.

The teacher is part of a fixed and defined system, an asymmetrical relationship in which their positional authority over the student is reinforced and supported in their school environment and in their teaching. However, it is in the implicit acceptance of the teacher/student relation and position that is not articulated but assumed and embedded; this calls for some form of recognition of individual hard work and achievement of the teacher. Showing gratitude to the individual teachers makes explicit their efforts to support students in a context of implicit and assumed relationships and work.

If positional authority is assumed and given, a teacher does not have to work as hard to achieve respect through authority with their students. Therefore, a different form of respect through individual gratitude from students is sought. Teachers' need for reciprocal gratitude from their students makes flexible the rigidity of their positional authority. They are now receiving from the student in a relationship in which the student has previously been the main recipient. However, this reaffirms their asymmetrical relationship, confirming the positional distance between teacher and student in which the teacher knows everything and the student, who was previously ignorant and unaware, is now aware and grateful to their teacher for their wisdom and guidance.

The need for students to show gratitude acknowledges the individual effort of the teacher and demonstrates their impact on student learning. Their active role within the lives of their students can bring about a sense of agency in which aspirations are shaped to their professional role and personal affirmation. Although, personal aspirations for these teachers were adjusted and their passive role accepted in childhood, their role as teachers supports active involvement in professional aspirations through their relationship with their students. They gain a sense of achievement through the gratitude and recognition of their individual efforts taken to ensure student success.

The impact of teacher affirmation on freedom of choice

Teachers' responses found that communal achievement included the family and the teacher in shared achievement of student success. Amu and Bhargavi described their satisfaction from hearing former students who attributed exam success to them as consequence of following their teacher's guidance. Bhargavi used recalled speech to emphasise verbal interaction with students and illustrate their relationship. This reveals in part, the basis on which their underlying concern with student acknowledgement acts as a form of return for their deontological commitment.

Success at school consolidates and confirms the teacher's efficacy and role in students' lives. This extends beyond economic emancipation of the student's family to reaffirming the teacher's role in helping them and acknowledging their care.

Teachers outlined care as central to their role, related to Noddings' (Noddings, 2003; Bergman, 2004) caring ideal, where the carer loses themselves through motivational displacement from themselves to those being cared for. This correlates to teachers' descriptions of their role as helping students through selfless concern for their wellbeing yet needing students to acknowledge not just their selfless care but attribute their success to the teacher's hard work. Student acknowledgement is much needed to centralise the teacher's role in their personal achievement. Teachers are prioritised within the classroom environment, where they are active and student passive. Their active participation and involvement in student achievement extend Noddings' caring relation to look at care as a form of transaction, in which the investment of the teacher necessitates a return of some kind, in this context to maintain a sense of teacher efficacy as key contributor of knowledge within the classroom.

In relation to Carr (Carr, 2005, 2006), for whom the teacher realises their own good through concern for others, teachers are made aware of their effectiveness through verbal acknowledgment of students. The teacher's care and concern for her students follows an asymmetric relationship, in which the teacher directs or instructs, and the students listen or follow. Care is demonstrated through instruction and takes on a distinctly maternal role. As mentioned previously, teachers used their role to put forward a maternal, gendered relation with their students, to care for them as a mother would, encouraging, disciplining, and utilising a maternal relation to build a relationship that used their gender as women.

Teachers' need for student acknowledgement could reverse this asymmetric relationship, where their concern is appreciated and position as teacher-carer affirmed. This is not an equitable balancing out of needs between teacher and student, where the teacher needs a student as much as the student needs a teacher. Instead, the strict, directive nature of the teacher–student relationship is reaffirmed and justified through student appreciation and acknowledging the teacher's positional power and care.

Higgins (Higgins, 2003) stated that focusing on their self-improvement may prevent teacher burn-out, enabling teachers to focus on their own interests to help students. The need for teachers to request student acknowledgement can be seen as a form of self-interest that prevents burn-out, preserving their sense of self within the demand to care selflessly for their students. This is seen in Celina's description of her depression following student failure. Celina expressed disappointment but approached this through explanations of ill health, rather than look at improving her teaching methods. Self-improvement was to amend her daily routine and medication.

Celina's dependence on student acknowledgement supports her own sense of success when students succeed. But when they fail, her sense of failure centres on external factors such as her health and not issues with her teaching. Her primary motivation may be to preserve her teaching status and sense of efficacy, especially when describing failure to an outsider. Here, self-interest may be delineated by a culture that demands selfless maternal care and assumes positional authority within the role of a female teacher.

To acknowledge internal failure and the need for self-improvement conflicts with expectations of teacher behaviour and efficacy. Teachers described student failure as being an individual act, as consequence of students not following their instruction. This may be where communal effort and the selfless care of the teacher is limited. The student must be a willing participant in instruction and passive recipient of the teacher's care and action. By not following the teacher, the student removes themselves from her care and is responsible for their own failure. They are required to motivate themselves to put in extra hours to study, including developing resilience to maintain concentration and attention. They are to be focused on achieving their academic goals and overcoming a difficult and testing period in their education. Attitudes and fundamental values surrounding achievement and teacher–student interaction place equal responsibility on the student to engage with their teacher to ensure success and not be responsible for their failure.

Knowledge production and transformation

Vijaysimha's (Vijaysimha, 2013) empirical study on how science textbooks were used in Indian classrooms revealed varying degrees of use depending on the type of school. Teachers relied upon textbooks to disseminate information more strongly in low-income government schools than in private or international schools. Further, knowledge was divided between what was required to learn in school and everyday knowledge outside of school.

Aligned with Vijaysimha (2013), teachers' responses emphasised the textbook when describing their teaching methods and student learning. The authority prescribed by the textbook supports the teacher's verbal explanation and influences student acceptance of textbook knowledge and teacher explanation. Vijaysimha examines the textbook as representation of the guru–shishya relationship from which the teacher's role is eroded to disseminate textbook knowledge to the student. My research extends the historical and cultural significance of the textbook attributed to the guru–shishya relationship, to consider the dynamics of interaction between teacher and student, in which roles are clearly defined and authority underwritten. Accepting teacher authority that is founded on the authority of the textbook is put forward here as a distributed personhood of knowledge.

In relation to Dewey and Habermas (Dewey, 2011; Campbell et al, 2004; Dill, 2007; Lovat, 2013), Dewey advocated that teachers should foster inquiry among their students rather than making them disciples of their authority. Habermas outlined critical self-reflexivity from empirical knowledge to comparative and authentic knowledge. Teachers' responses here indicated that knowledge was reproduced in the textbook that was predesigned, then filtered and distributed by the teacher. The authority of such knowledge arises from the subject textbook designed and sanctioned by the state government and from which summative exam papers are based and answers proscribed. This contributes to an epistemology of knowledge production as one that is primarily distributed and defined by statives of what should be known and understood by the student. To critique or question such knowledge would be to undermine this distributed personhood of knowledge and its authenticity.

The teacher is key negotiator between the textbook as the body of knowledge, communicating what is to be learnt or understood to the student. The teacher explains the text while maintaining its overall authority. The teacher's authority is derived from the authority of the text and as part of the distributed personhood of knowledge through text and teacher explanation.

In relation to Habermas's authentic knowledge as derived from empirical and comparative knowledge, the authenticity of the knowledge source is significant, depending on who provides knowledge and where it comes from, rather than authenticity derived from individual observation and comparison, such as Giddens's (1991) morality of authenticity. This research proposes that authenticity within the

Figure 4.4: Distributed personhood of knowledge and authority within the Indian classroom

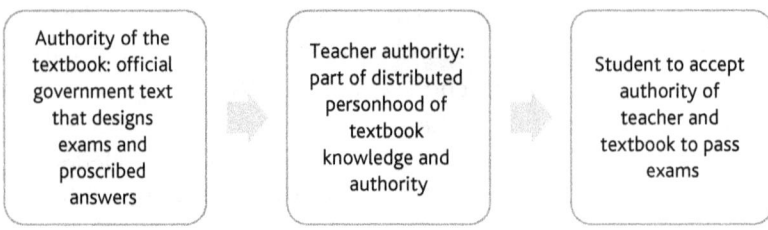

Indian context is subsumed into notions of authority (see Figure 4.4). Knowledge production, therefore, results in derivatives and imitations of textbook and teacher knowledge, a necessary function to pass exams that require students to reproduce such knowledge.

Research into the teacher identity within India put forward the dominance of the guru–shishya (teacher–student/disciple) model in which the guru acted out of charity and goodwill towards their student to pass on their knowledge and skills (Mlecko, 1982; Sarangapani, 2003; Smail, 2013; Batra, 2014; Ganapathy-Coleman, 2014). Distributed personhood of knowledge, like the guru–shishya model, reflects the relationship values between teacher and student. However, the cultural precedent of the guru was not specifically referred to by teachers. Teacher authority and knowledge distribution emerged through descriptions of their roles and responsibilities. The guru–shishya model is not immediately apparent within the daily routine of teaching and learning in the classroom. Rather it serves as a means of Indian education research to understand sources and causal factors for Indian teacher–student interaction and identity.

Description, narrative, and statives in disseminating knowledge

Teachers used description and narratives to communicate what they believed, understood and enacted within their personal and professional lives. What should be done, how it should be carried out, what is expected of them and of others, defined rules and regulations that put across a sense of order related to their teaching practice. Narratives were part of recall or the act of remembering, described through stories, actions and examples. The 'narrative' or story itself that teachers told acted as an explanation of a point that they were making, as possible metaphor to support a statement with no further explanation or analysis required. The narrative or story that served as explanation essentially became a statement without any explanation or depth. This relates to the guru–shishya model, with the teacher not needing to offer further explanation of information or knowledge. The story or description is put forward as an explanation of abstract connections that are not to be questioned by the student but which embodies 'knowledge' to be imbibed. Their authority stems from statives of what a student should know and what constitutes knowledge itself.

Teachers' use of description and narratives as statements limits their understanding of the social and cultural foundations of their beliefs and values. For low-income female teachers, relying on description and narrative as explanation re-enacts an authoritative model of the historic guru–shishya by repeating metaphors, stories that are to be accepted by the student and not queried any further. This takes place within a context in which their teaching is not necessarily an act of charity, as it is with the guru, and they may not be part of a higher caste with social and cultural affirmation. Hence, teacher affirmation for low-income female teachers may be derived from a more rigid performance of authority when disseminating knowledge through description, narrative and stative verbs. Distributed personhood of knowledge for these teachers is supported by relying on description, stories and statives of what students must know to support teachers' teaching and dissemination of knowledge.

Student achievement and transformation as act of teacher creativity

Teachers emphasised summative learning as a key indicator of student learning. Success at exams indicates the student has reached a certain state, in which distributed knowledge has been successfully received. The exam acts as a test of what they have learnt, resulting from their transformation at the hands of their teacher.

Teachers' responses found a distinction between knowledge needed to pass exams, everyday practical knowledge, and knowledge taught through teaching of values, which is a more personal and invested act of transformation by the teacher. The transformative act of teaching is where the teacher acts as builder, enabling a student to reach a certain stage to pass exams or guided by morals and values inculcated by the teacher. Teaching is action that builds relationships, values and knowledge. The act of construction and not destruction ties in with conflict avoidance demonstrated by teachers in Chapter 3.

In addition to maintaining social cohesion and relation, there was a distinct move for teachers to outline themselves as those who did not cause conflict in comparison to those who might – those parents or management who criticise them. This further underlines their role as builder, of being constructive and making positive relationships and positive action with a goal of bringing transformation to the student.

This relates to Carr's (Campbell et al, 2004; Carr, 2005, 2006) ideal phronesis of the teacher to advocate and commit to a student as an individual and future member of society, an act that requires the teacher to possess the values being taught. Teaching values could ensure social relation and maintain authority of knowledge. The teacher as builder extends Carr's avocation of teachers possessing values to teachers as active agents in inculcating and helping to construct values within the student, that is from possessing and disseminating values to constructing them.

Freire (1996) outlines the inherent distrust by oppressors that the oppressed can think for themselves, rather than relying on oppressors to make them reflect and open themselves to look at their inherent prejudices and attitudes. The teacher, in helping the student towards self-efficacy and independent thinking, should examine the entangled space in which foundations of authority and asymmetrical relationships are embedded. Teachers' responses here are not consistent with Freire's notion of the self-examination of prejudices and attitudes, including helping the student towards self-efficacy and independent thinking. These are not values that are taught or drawn upon in the Indian classroom. Reflective practice and independent thinking are not aims for teachers within their everyday practice, despite being part of the BEd syllabus.

For teachers, distrust lies in the student's lack of capability in constructing themselves. They require the teacher, who has been directed by their own parents, to construct values for them. Self-efficacy is not transformation; rather transformation is externally directed and controlled, the act of creation and construction rather than self-actualisation.

Teacher values within transformation place the teacher as central to student learning and defines their social praxis and action. Authentic knowledge is defined by values associated with authenticity and authority of knowledge contained within the textbook that in turn sets exam questions and answers. A distributed personhood of knowledge is enacted through the teacher's verbal explanations, reinforcing their authenticity and positional authority as intermediary between the textbook and student. The use of description, narrative and statives are key elements in defining values related to teacher authority within this context. By limiting knowledge to description, narratives and statives, students are less likely to question and query information being delivered, thus extending teachers' positional authority in controlling and disseminating knowledge to students. Description and delivery of textbook information act as a form of classroom control, placing the teacher as interpreter of government sanctioned textbooks that cannot be understood by students without the teacher's descriptions.

Teachers' attitudes to transformation are founded on their understanding of achievement and how an authentic knowledge contributes to this (see Figure 4.4). Authentic knowledge is both authenticated through the authority of textbooks that are needed to pass exams and knowledge defined by personal values that teachers feel important to disseminate to students. Central to teachers' attitudes to transformation is their active role in transforming the lives of their students.

Transformation occurs as a consequence of the constructive act of teaching. There are clear separations of roles within the teacher–student relationship, with the teacher as instigating learning and bringing about transformation through constructing and building the student. The teacher is placed as having a strong moral educator role, with students needing to be constructed by them. Transformation in this context, and therefore also social action, is defined as using a teacher's individual understanding of what students need to know. Central to authentic knowledge and transformation are values surrounding notions of student efficacy, in which academic and economic achievement including moral discipline are defined by external instruction. Authentic, authoritative knowledge and transformation arise through the teacher's voice in the classroom. An understanding of transformation is delineated by a teacher's moral educator role and occurs as part of communal action between teacher and student.

Implications for reflective practice in teacher education

Distributed personhood of knowledge has significant implications for developing reflective practice as it underlines attitudes to knowledge and continual learning. It would be useful for trainees to examine their own values in relation to being a teacher: what constitutes knowledge for them and what are the foundations of values they believe important to pass onto students?

Training may need to address the motivations and intentions of trainees entering the teaching profession as not straightforward nor comprising solely of altruistic motivations to better the lives of students. Rather, the choice to teach may result from financial motivations, a convenient job that enables a female teacher to look after their family including work, or a more socially accepted position that is more female-oriented compared with working in the mixed-gender environment of an office. It is important that training enables trainee teachers to explore their own personal and professional aspirations and understanding of achievement. This is more suited to training that examines the nature of teaching as a profession and the role of the teacher in relation to their student.

Training can help teachers further understand how speech has the potential to exercise a form of control over student learning and not just behaviour within the classroom. Training programmes that focus on developing independent learning through adapting the teacher's speech and reliance on stative descriptions and restrictive illustrations are valuable within institutions in which resources are often limited to the teacher, a blackboard and a textbook.

Central to adapting verbal speech is examining the interpretive role of the teacher who reiterates textbook material to students. Adapting one's speech to allow for student interpretation and explanation could help counter the active/passive role of teacher and student. Open questioning is not necessarily applicable here, as asking a student what they think or what their ideas are about a topic relies on prior established practice within classrooms of developing active student participation in discussions. This may occur in Indian classrooms but is not consistent practice across the school system and certainly not within low-income schools where rote teaching is prevalent. Training can help enable teachers to adopt more analytical and discursive speech to act as a guide to encourage student verbal analysis and discursive skills.

Trainees could be asked to consider why they use certain words or descriptions and what they hope to put across, in training programmes that focus on their choice of words. A focus on words emphasises the value of verbal communication as pedagogically significant for both student and peer relationships and teaching technique. The primacy of language – of words, speech and spoken syntax – are bound together and can significantly impact understanding one's teaching and role as educator.

5

Conclusion

This chapter concludes the main discussion within the preceding chapters and outlines implications for teacher education in India (see Figure 5.1). It highlights the need for understanding female empowerment and agency in India as one that works within social and communal expectations of women and that is culturally and socially astute to power and positional authority.

The chapter concludes with my reflections on the context of conducting social justice research in this way, in particular my position as advocate including being an outsider in relation to teachers.

Agency within teacher roles, social spaces and attitudes to transformation

Agency through determining place among others

Social relationships within a context of agency are rooted in relational agency: agency is determined through understanding one's position in relation to others. In the terms of interviewees Amu, Celina, Deepa and Bhargavi, social relationships relate to how one impacts another through mutual relationships. Positionality and relational agency comprise not just one's position within a hierarchical social structure, but are also determined by the active influence one has over another as validated and determined by such structures (see Figure 5.2). For teachers, their positional authority over students is validated by their role as teachers. However, it is the teachers' direction of learning, behaviour and partaking in collective achievement of their students

Figure 5.1: Chapter 5 outline

Figure 5.2: Agency within teacher roles, social spaces and attitudes to transformation

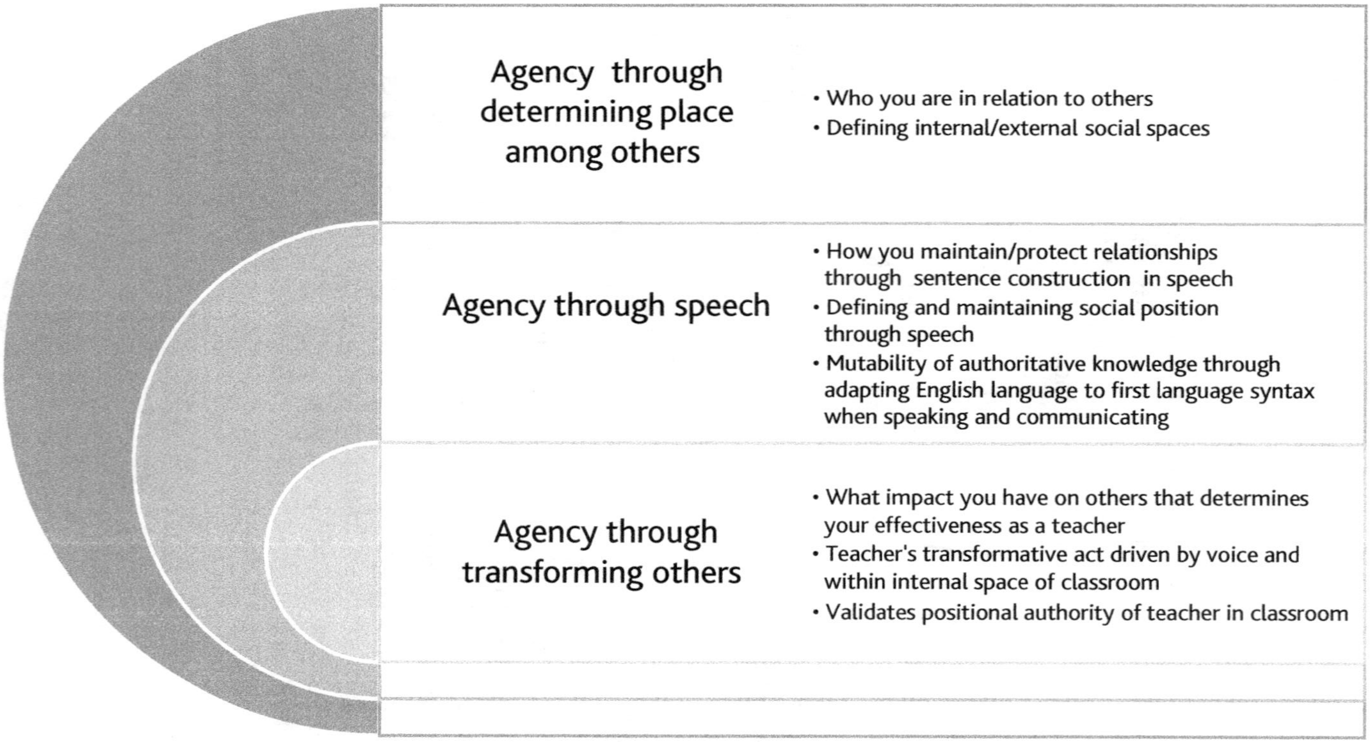

Agency through determining place among others
- Who you are in relation to others
- Defining internal/external social spaces

Agency through speech
- How you maintain/protect relationships through sentence construction in speech
- Defining and maintaining social position through speech
- Mutability of authoritative knowledge through adapting English language to first language syntax when speaking and communicating

Agency through transforming others
- What impact you have on others that determines your effectiveness as a teacher
- Teacher's transformative act driven by voice and within internal space of classroom
- Validates positional authority of teacher in classroom

that places their agency as deeply rooted in their immediate and direct act of influence over their students.

Agency through speech in navigating social spaces

Talking about internal and external social spaces revealed female teachers used their speech to manage representation within these spaces. Social spaces outlined the pervasiveness of society, particularly in relation to gender. Teachers' use of linguistic negotiation revealed the significance of speech in enabling agency. This was highlighted in teachers' use of assertive and defensive positioning when responding to questions. This included using the English language as a subject to be taught to students but adapted to fit in with the sentence structure of teachers' first language when used to communicate. This indicated a shift between taught knowledge as immutable and representative of external authority, such as written English language rules disseminated from a textbook, and knowledge that is functional and adapted in practice, as when teachers adjusted English language sentence structure in their immediate verbal speech.

The act of translation between first and second language also suggests teachers demonstrated choice when putting forward a particular perspective or image to protect their collective identity to an outsider researcher.

Through practical application of the English language, through translation and communication, how teachers adapted and constructed their speech indicates a clear command of representation through words. It is this act of adaptation – of reconstruction and the ability to manoeuvre out of the authoritarian rules of a language that they themselves teach to students – that demonstrate the foundation and beginnings of agency.

Agency through transformative action on others

Attitudes to transformation examined the role knowledge played in achievement and social emancipation, and the teacher's role within this. What is considered 'authentic knowledge' was related to notions of external authority of knowledge and teacher positionality. Authentic knowledge was defined by what a student should know or should be taught. The textbook issued by the educational authority represented external authority, with the teacher as interpreter and disseminator of textbook knowledge. Attitudes to capability and achievement for students and teachers revealed a discrepancy between what teachers viewed as achievement, relating to securing future success, and personal, individual achievement, relating to a meaningful life rooted in happiness, parental security and good health. Fundamental to their role, teachers emphasised their role as builder, constructing capability in students to be successful in their future, determined and enabled through academic achievement including moral education.

It is within this moral educator role that teachers highlighted their personal investment in students. Moral education required they provide direction beyond that of the textbook, to use their own understanding of civic responsibility, morality and ethics which they pass on to students. Enabling students to pass exams was not as significant as their act of transformation in the holistic development of the student. Agency in this context is defined by teachers' transformative action in enabling students to be prepared for future success and contribution to society. The transformative act of teachers is one in which they construct: they build and act as the foundation for their students' future success and achievements. Here lies a key conflict within this examination of low-income female teacher agency. The act of agency in which a marginalised group of low-income female teachers enact upon their students is at odds with the consequences of such action on the agency of students themselves to construct or develop their own learning. Low-income female teachers may locate agency through their transformation of students, but it is this very 'act of transformation' that sits within the hand of the teacher and not the student, that conflicts and contradicts the nature of agency itself. Agency based on such acts of transformation is entangled within teachers' positional authority, validated by their interpreter role of external authority when disseminating government textbook knowledge to students. Although this provides significant authority and status to female teachers who may not receive such authority within their personal lives, it reproduces unequal structures in which the student is disenabled from agency. It is important to understand the classroom context in which agency occurs for these teachers in order to examine the complexities involved in self-determination and independence of learning for students.

The classroom as a space for female teacher empowerment

Agency of low-income female teachers in Bangalore, India, is defined by their relationships with others. Teachers' sense of self, of who they

Figure 5.3: The classroom as a space for female teacher agency

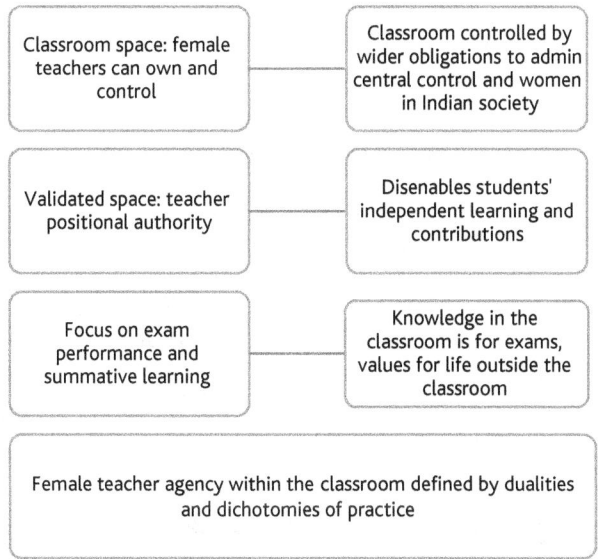

are, is embedded within the social structure of which they are a part. Their agency or acts of agency tend to be implicit and enacted through linguistic negotiation of their speech, determining who they are in relation to others and exercising positional authority through their teaching and moral educator role. The need continually to consider or factor in those around them in their professional roles indicates the pervasiveness of collective identity and relational agency, even though their descriptions of teaching are singular and individual. They are on their own with students in a classroom yet still part of a wider set of obligations and expectations that extend beyond their professional roles as teachers and are founded in their roles as women in Indian society (see Figure 5.3).

The classroom as a space for empowerment is a key area where an understanding of agency for these teachers is examined. The idea of the classroom as a space in which teachers can command and direct students' learning and behaviour is supported by societal relationships outside the classroom. These validate teachers' ownership of the classroom as a distinct space which women are allowed to own or be authoritative in. As outlined by Ramachandran (2000, 2003), low income women's contribution to the household was relegated to domestic duties and caring for livestock and their land ownership rights were restricted. In terms of female teachers within low-income schools, the classroom acts as a similarly validated space, with similar duties of maternal care and instruction as part of their professional responsibilities. Although female teachers are in command of their classroom, they do so as part of socially validated authority and space as female teachers. They are salaried workers but within roles that are socially accepted and fit within obligations to care for family and children.

They possess positional authority in relation to their students, but this is limited to being an interpreter of government-issued textbooks which possess external authority. This highlights the context in which female teachers operate and which may lead them to negotiate agency through speech.

India itself is a place where one negotiates or navigates around others, whether it be in the manner one addresses another, the physical space to move around or walk in crowded cities, or one's monetary, legal and societal rights (Ramachandran, 2000, 2003; Jandhyala and Ramachandran, 2009; Kumar, 2010). The social and cultural contexts in which female teachers operate are underwritten by a need to negotiate between what is expected of you and what you can be or do, to find a way through or negotiate a path while considering those around you. Just as they pick their way through a crowded road or pavement, female teachers continually negotiate within their personal and professional lives towards a form of self-determination that adjusts the internal and external social spaces in which they are embedded. This is especially pertinent for low-income female teachers, who do not have the economic status and power to exercise positional authority afforded by a higher income and social status.

The classroom may be a space in which teachers' authority is validated, but their act of teaching and transformation disenables their students to construct their own learning. Comparing being given command of a classroom and authority to teach students with the actual practice of disseminating information from textbook to students reveals a discrepancy between the appearance of authority and the practice of it. As found with teachers' use of English language, a dichotomy exists: what is taught to students in terms of what should be known contrasts with what is practised and adapted through use, through function.

It is this dichotomy that is most interesting when attempting to understand agency for low-income female teachers in Indian society, in particular the difference in approach to what should be known, what should be taught as immutable authoritative knowledge and the significance of such knowledge in everyday life. As examined in Chapter 4, teachers distinguished between academic achievement to secure future education towards social and economic emancipation and the skills needed to run a successful business for financial security. There is a difference between what one should do and know and what happens outside the classroom. Teachers placed greater emphasis on what students must know, of student attention towards their teacher, following instructions and repeating phrases back to check learning. This demonstrates teacher control, command and, most importantly, their efficacy in relation to expected duties of what a teacher must be able to do within a classroom.

The social realities that exist outside the classroom are described by teachers, but as areas that are outside their control. These are the influx of immigrant communities from neighbouring states, and the breakdown of family structure with both parents working and its consequences for rising rape culture. This itself is a form of negotiation. This dichotomy or duality of expected roles and actions crucially informs the learning culture that students grow up in and are part of within their future professional lives. Duality between what should be done to fulfil immediate expectations within the classroom, office and home and what takes place outside is established within the classroom. It defines students' approach to self-determination, independent thinking and self-actualisation for the rest of their lives. They are taught to follow instructions without an indication of what those instructions will contribute towards or lead to. Knowledge and skills are needed to fulfil immediate aims of passing an exam that does not support future application of such knowledge or skills: this has significant implications for lifelong learning and professional capability and development.

For students within low-income schools, resources to develop knowledge and skills beyond the classroom are limited as families often do not possess a laptop or share a single smartphone between them. This further disenables students from gaining or seeking employment where they are not reduced to following their employer's instructions or a script of duties and actions. These are effectively forms of manual labour, whether it is physical manual labour comprising both skilled and unskilled labour, or technical labour within a call centre that is based on processes, instructions and a script to workers. Low-income female teacher agency impacts not only the agency of teachers but students' agency around lifelong learning that could support better education opportunities and economic stability.

It is crucial that discourse surrounding female teacher identity in India considers how such teachers negotiate expectations from their role as mother, daughter, wife and sister to be disseminators of knowledge and its impact on the students they teach. In particular, such discourse must consider the reproduction of a learning culture in which one navigates what is expected of them in the classroom with what they can do outside the classroom. This may be true in all cultures in which there is a discrepancy between theory and practical knowledge. However, within the specific cultural context in which these teachers and students are embedded, the need to negotiate what one can do (Morrow, 2013) is prevalent in all aspects of an individual's life. The learning culture that teachers contribute to and its impact on students' ability to navigate future employment and economic survival need to be examined if education policy aims of developing a generation of Indian citizens who contribute to society and achieve global standards of attainment and education are to be met. It is important that the dichotomy of practice within and outside the classroom in relation to a teacher's role, student performance and attainment is considered in relation to the subsequent capability of students and teachers to determine and achieve aspirations.

Therefore, the classroom as a space for female teacher empowerment is made complex in the restrictions placed on teachers to act as interpreter of external authentic knowledge, and for whom command and control are linked to teacher efficacy and behaviour. The classroom affirms their status as teacher but restricts their authority to that which is given to them. This reveals the need for teachers to emphasise their act of transformation – of building up and constructing a student – as positive action that affirms their individual effectiveness as a teacher. 'What should be known' as directed by external authority also indicates what a teacher should be teaching or doing in the classroom and as a marker for their effectiveness. In continually adjusting and negotiating with those around them, teachers assess their efficacy in relation to what is expected of them, as they lack means and ways to assess tffectffectiveness outside of proscribed duties and responsibilities.

There is a real need for reflective practice that emphasises individual assessment of teacher efficacy in relation to their impact on student learning as opposed to following predetermined rules and regulations that have minimal practical application within the realities of the classroom.

Reworking teacher effectiveness and consequences for reflective practice in teacher education in India

Reflective practice requires assessing one's teaching in relation to a criterion of effectiveness. This may refer to institutional, pedagogical criteria, including the impact of one's teaching on student learning and development. It is an area which is foundational for teacher education programmes across the world and, significantly, within higher education institutions that provide such training. Reflective practice enables problem identification, reflective analysis and the highlighting of areas to be improved. The basis of reflective practice for teachers is continual development facilitated by continually evaluating one's effectiveness during and after teaching or contact with students. This is driven by a need to improve one's teaching for the benefit of students. Reflective practice in India is an area of some complexity; research projects have found that teachers did not possess the skills or time to identify problems with their teaching (Dyer et al, 2004). As discussed in Chapter 1, the emphasis on reflective practice within education in India is primarily theoretical and not based on the active practical skills that are at the heart of reflective practice within any industry or sector. It is the exercise and practical application of experiential, work-based learning in which the realities of one's practice of teaching are mediated and examined through reflection on key events and experiences.

A key focus of reflective analysis for teachers is the assessment of one's effectiveness as a teacher in relation to teaching methods and approach: in essence, are the methods used by a teacher – to teach a particular subject, design materials, or engage students – effective in helping students to understand and meet their learning outcomes? Emphasising what a teacher should do or is expected to do takes away from the actual practice of what a teacher does in the classroom or the quality of their teaching in terms of supporting students to understand and engage with the content of their lessons. The roots of such emphasis may be found in a colonial foundation of didactic behaviourist education (Kumar, 1988, 2011) and are reproduced through the facilitator role proscribed by child-centred education policies.

However, it is this focus on preparation, on the need to construct or 'build' teachers before they enter the classroom, that reinforces the same behaviourist model of teaching and learning in which the student, be they student or student-teacher, is empty till they are filled up with knowledge. At its core is the contradiction of immutable knowledge that has minimal impact or practical application in real life. It is there to fulfil a purpose, to tick boxes and check against a list of what should be known. Hence learning outcomes for lessons are either impractical or focused on memorisation of textbook content with information as the ultimate objective, to pass summative exams that determine student learning. If teacher effectiveness is based on the fulfilment of expected duties, resultant student exam performance is not part of this framework of effectiveness. This could be why teachers interviewed considered student failure as separate to their effectiveness.

It would be useful to examine three key areas in which teacher effectiveness could be approached or considered by teacher education within India: first, effectiveness through an understanding of teacher expertise and its foundations with constructivist approaches to teaching; second, the emotional investment and practice of teaching; and third, an examination of teacher education for social justice.

Teacher effectiveness as teacher expertise

Hattie (Hattie, 2003) outlines that a key aspect of teachers who make a difference is the quality of their teaching and its impact on student variance and achievement. Conflating teacher expertise with experience restricts teaching expertise to longevity of service and does not emphasise or reward skills and quality of teaching. Hattie put forward an understanding of teacher expertise as having a clearer and detailed understanding of the context in which learning occurs. This may take place in the teacher's unique knowledge of their students; this includes: being aware of varying levels of learning in the classroom, problem solving and adapting teaching as needed, encouraging deep learning and higher order thinking, as well as being effective in prioritising and making decisions on teaching content, delivery and assessment of methods. The expert teacher does not need to have several years of experience to develop such skills, but does need a deeper, more contextualised understanding of the learning environment and how students learn.

This is supported by a constructivist approach to teaching (Biggs, 1996), in which the student is central to the creation of meaning within the classroom. They support their learning by actively selecting and constructing their knowledge through individual and social activities that support such learning. As with Hattie's outline of expertise, teaching is part of a complex system in which classroom, teacher, students, context, activities and outcome are integrated and interrelated. Biggs outlines that the key difference between 'surface learning' and 'deep learning' is based on the ability of the student to make decisions. Teaching that supports students to review and explain content or look for relationships between different sources of knowledge still reproduces the dominance of 'knowledge'. It does not enable students to discern the nature of knowledge or of the content being studied as the basis for critical thinking and development of metacognitive skills. Instead, it prioritises what a student should be able to do through their engagement in learning activities that support their individual construction of knowledge. Biggs' impact on education has been singular in his outline of constructive alignment that aligns learning activities with assessment through learning outcomes. Students' construction of learning is supported by aligning learning activities to support assessment, through designing learning outcomes to focus on what students should be able to demonstrate at varying levels of understanding.

In terms of teaching within an Indian context, constructivism can, at first glance, be at odds with an education system in which teacher authority disallows student construction of knowledge. Key to this is a misconception of constructivism that equates constructivist approaches to learning with student-centred learning as defined by child-centred education policies. Gordon (Gordon, 2009) outlines a misuse of constructivism as prioritising student learning and child-centred education in detriment to the role of the teacher within the classroom who supports learning through their subject matter knowledge. The emphasis on appropriate and supportive learning activities designed and prepared by the teacher signifies teachers' action within the classroom and their subject matter authority. Teachers use their understanding and knowledge of their subject not only to design activities but to support and correct student misconceptions. This necessitates a deep understanding of their subject and places them as a significant actor within the classroom (Richardson, 2003).

Constructivist approaches within teacher education in India may help support teacher authority in the classroom based on their subject expertise and ability to adapt content towards supporting higher order thinking through appropriate learning activities. This concurs with a cultural emphasis on subject/content expertise but one made active, through the teacher employing their subject knowledge skills to design teaching that supports active learning as opposed to the banking of knowledge with no future application or purpose. This does mean that teachers need to be encouraged to reconsider their relationship with their textbooks. If they are to design active learning activities, textbook material would act as facilitator rather than ultimate authority in the classroom. Teachers' subject knowledge is crucial for effective teaching, calling into question the dual degree programme of two years of a subject specialism and two years of a BEd. Teachers with reduced access to developing subject knowledge that supports effective teaching are disadvantaged in being able to design effective activities and may resort to textbook guidance to support their teaching.

It is important to note that constructivist principles in teacher education are more effective and beneficial for in-service teachers who are in the classroom and able to reflect on their daily teaching. Immediate, direct experience offers an opportunity to review one's actions within the specific context in which they occurred and build insights incrementally into practice (White, 2002).

If constructivist principles are integrated within teacher education in India, it may be useful to support teachers based on their individual understanding of their subject and ability to support student learning activities. To embed constructivism within teacher education, it is important to factor in the emotional investment they place within their students.

Teacher effectiveness as emotional investment

Hargreaves (Hargreaves, 1998) called for education reform within the UK to consider teaching as emotional practice. The importance of teachers' emotional relationship with students is key to their active participation and enthusiasm within the classroom. Hargreaves outlines emotional understanding and emotional labour as core elements of a teacher's skill in providing emotional support for students and defining teacher motivation. Power dynamics between teacher and student work against the teacher's ability to recognise and provide emotional support as well as restricting their emotional investment in their teaching.

The emotional aspect of teaching practice is supported by Zembylas's research on emotions as discursive practice in teaching (Zembylas, 2005). Zembylas uses Foucault's notion of power as process to approach teacher emotions as a product of complex power relations in which the teacher exercises emotional control and adheres to emotional rules. Zembylas argues that understanding the role of power in creating emotions places emotions as fundamental to teaching and teacher identity. These latter are to be approached discursively, as part of a deconstruction of power relations and its impact on emotions in teaching.

Hargreaves and Zembylas may have particular significance for female teachers in India, who are demonstratively emotionally invested in their students and for whom teaching is a decidedly emotional practice. However, given that maternal constructs of care and nurture are embedded within societal expectations of female teachers, individual and personal emotional relationships are difficult to separate and ascertain.

Teacher effectiveness based on their emotional relationship with students can support reflective practice in enabling teachers to locate their reflections within descriptions of emotional connections with students and their teaching practice. However, it is an area in which expected emotional investment is culturally and socially defined. Although useful as a starting point for reflective practice, the ability to step back and evaluate one's emotional investment from an objective, critical lens that necessitates reflective analysis may be fraught with complexities in which gendered references to care are reproduced. This itself may be useful for teacher educators to note and support trainee teachers to unpack. Given the teacher's commitment to student transformation, it may be possible to consider teaching effectiveness using emotional investment in students in relation to social justice.

Teacher effectiveness as social justice action

Cochran-Smith (Cochran-Smith, 2010) puts forward a theory of justice, practice and teacher preparation as interrelated elements that support teacher education for social justice. She defines social justice as supporting the equity of learning opportunities for all groups in society, respect for all social groups, and acknowledging and dealing with tensions in which injustice occurs. A primary purpose for teacher education is to support teachers in prioritising student learning and enhancing their life chances. This helps create rich and real learning opportunities for students, with the teacher as advocate and activist of social injustices within the classroom. Bhargavi and Deepa advocated for student learning outside of exam performance while recognising the realities of such achievement for future success. This highlights the complex nature of teacher as activist and advocate within a system that works against or disenables this role.

Cochran-Smith's notion of teacher education for social justice may seem impossible to fulfil here, as low-income female teachers themselves are subject to and embedded within unequal social structures. However, the teacher as transformative through their advocate role may be possible if linked to their caring and nurturing role within the classroom. Emotional investment placed within students can enable teachers in pre- and in-service training to explore their role as part of wider systems to enact social change. Teachers did indicate their awareness of social realities through descriptions of generic social issues, such as breakdown in family structures or the growth of rape culture as a product of girls being left alone at home due to both parents working.

Examining teacher effectiveness in terms of their social justice roles is made complex when teachers perpetuate inequalities themselves within their classroom. This may be an area that requires further, careful consideration, as examining structural inequalities can have a wider impact on low-income female teacher identity beyond the classroom.

Akkerman and Meijer's examination of the dialogical self in relation to teacher identity puts forward the idea that teachers' self can be viewed through the interrelation of multiple 'I-positions' that define teachers' personal and professional lives (Akkerman and Meijer, 2011). These consist of postmodern and modern constructions of self that are in tandem, such as multiple/unitary selves, discontinuous/continuous selves, and social/individual selves. These indicate the negotiation of multiple I-positions towards maintaining oneself within one's working life. In essence, the self is a space where negotiation between different multiple I-positions takes place, defined through 'Who I am at this moment' to respond to any context at any time. It is not defragmented identity as such, but a move towards coherence and consistency in response to any given situation. Akkerman and Meijer put forward that such complexities of identity are an ongoing process of self-dialogue and negotiation with social and individual factors. Self-narratives draw out ambiguities within teacher identity. An understanding of self as dialogical is useful to support reflective practice within teacher education in India; teachers could examine who they are within the different roles they occupy. However, the use of self-narratives may not work towards highlighting ambiguities as intended by Akkerman and Meijer, as those ambiguities may be hidden and might threaten female teacher stability if surfaced.

What is interesting is the move towards teacher identity, motivations and practice as fundamentally complex. The focus on complexity of teaching practice is quite different to that indicated by Amu, Celina, Bhargavi and Deepa. For them, the complexities of their roles are implicit or tacitly understood (Clarke, 2001) and culturally defined. The implications of reflective practice within teacher education in India to make explicit that which is implicit in an individual's personal and professional lives have distinct consequences for the low-income female teacher within India. It is not an area that one should go into without careful consideration of the impact of such reflection and the security and social structures in which teachers are not only embedded but reliant.

Teacher effectiveness provides ways for teachers to assess their own teaching based on the realities of everyday, daily events in the classroom and grounded in the actual context of teaching. This helps move away from predetermined rules of teaching effectiveness in which the teacher is a component of a system – a top-down policy that has minimal bearing on actual teaching within the classroom and the personal and professional lives of its teachers.

Explicit and visible agency

Clarke's significant (Clarke, 2001) research into teacher identity in Bangalore examined the social and cultural impact on teacher thinking and pedagogy using explicit and implicit cultural models. These underline self-expressed reflection and acted-out praxis as well as implicit cultural models as interpreted by the author. Clarke's research located teachers' thinking within the social and cultural contexts that direct their pedagogy, putting forward a culturally embedded perspective of teacher thinking and pedagogical practice. This is a highly significant text in relation to my research and aligns with the relationship between implicit social and cultural models and the difficulties or complexities in bringing them to the surface within reflective practice for teachers. However, I propose an alternate focus regarding the dominance of cultural and social constructs within a teacher's life. I agree that teachers are, to an extent, products of their cultural or social environments as they do reproduce dominant ideas and attitudes in their responses. However, I do not believe we need to seek causal meaning to everything they say and do, where the uniqueness of the teacher's voice and words could be subsumed into larger constructs. Rather it is how teachers make and attribute meaning that is the imperative for this book; culture informs this process to a certain extent. There is value in the idiosyncratic action and primacy of the teacher and their individual acts of agency for teacher education.

Agency that takes place under the surface is specific to tacit ways of being, of living and working, especially if one is a low-income woman in India. How they protect themselves, choose their words, construct their language, or use their voice demonstrates their awareness of their social position and roles as female teachers. Agency for these teachers is the outcome of negotiating expectations and moving between I-positions (Akkerman and Meijer, 2011).

The tacit negotiation of self, unitary and multiple, is a result of moving between and meeting expectations. Yet the low-income female teacher in India is not a composite of multiple roles and expected duties. They are individuals who actively employ their speech to navigate their environment. Speech, which is individual to them and constructed by them, acts as the space for such agency. Therefore, teacher education reform must consider, in addition to teacher effectiveness, the contributions of speech and the crucial significance this has for low-income female teachers in engaging with and responding to expectations. The dynamic and interactive environment outlined by White (White, 2002) in her constructive approach to reflective practice is facilitated through an emphasis on teachers' speech, their main resource and tool used in the classroom and that in which they are adept at utilising (see Figure 5.4).

Figure 5.4: Explicit and visible agency through speech, as defined by negotiating between different expectations and roles

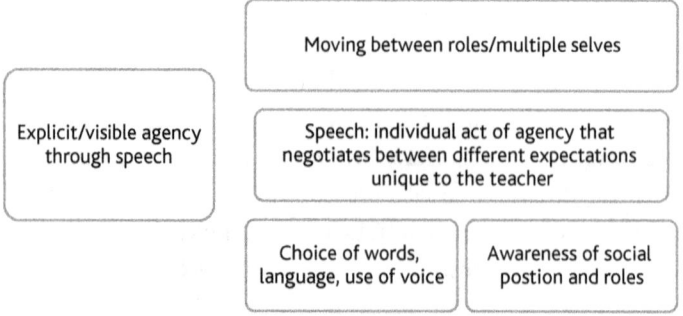

Need for reworking reflective practice in teacher education in India

It is crucially important for teacher education within India to reconsider not only how reflective practice is taught in BEd courses but also how teacher effectiveness is understood and communicated. If reflective practice units could emphasise the impact teachers have on student learning, it could help approach their effectiveness based on their classroom practice. Teachers are encouraged to consider what it means to be effective within the classroom. Although this could result in teachers reiterating student exam performance, classroom behaviour or their own length of service in their roles, it could help open discussion on perceived markers of effectiveness or teacher success.

At the heart of the need for teacher education reform is the lack of systems and structures that celebrate teacher effectiveness and success beyond student gratitude sought by teachers. Low-income female teachers are constructs of an educational system in which they facilitate students to prepare for exams and demonstrate understanding of external authoritative knowledge such as government-sanctioned textbooks. Being able to measure your effectiveness as a teacher by reflecting on your individual impact on student learning can help female teachers to determine efficacy outside of expected duties. This could further support teachers to build on their emotional investment in students, the agency they filter through their teaching as transformative action, or perspectives they have on freedom of choice, capability and achievement for them and their students.

Certainly, this may be an ideal scenario – and it is one which requires female teachers to feel secure enough to review both their teaching and their personal and professional lives. It is important that any new or innovative ways of introducing reflection or self-assessment consider how low-income female teachers view their roles and values within their teaching practice. These values lay the foundation for acts of agency that forge a path that is personal to them.

Child-centred education policies in India focus on the roles and duties of the teacher as facilitator. The lack of understanding and cultural fit of such policies has meant that teachers returned to behaviourist methods to fulfil exam performance criteria. A clearer outline of student-led teaching and learning could support teacher education programmes attempting to employ constructivist methods. This can only begin by teachers being encouraged to construct their learning through training opportunities, to experience and understand the differences between instructor-led and student-led teaching and to determine for themselves appropriate methods for their students in relation to their subject.

It is important to recognise that, while a significant pedagogical area that is widespread among Western educational institutions, constructivism and student-led learning do not necessarily translate to cultural contexts such as India. India's historical learning culture is primarily didactic and endemic to social structures and relationships, defining the teacher–student relationship. I do not stipulate the authoritative use of student-led learning or constructivism as a push towards individual and neoliberal freedom of choice as exhibited by Sen and Nussbaum (see Chapter 1). Rather, I propose the need for a ground-up approach to understanding teacher effectiveness: to lay bare the realities of the teacher's and student's role within the classroom and provide teachers with a criterion for affirmation and effectiveness that is not based on collective achievement. This could be in the act of teaching in the classroom, on the methods employed, and around the engagement and discussion they engender with students. It is about reviewing the criteria of what makes an effective teacher as a continual process of evaluation and development, laying the foundation for continuing professional development of teachers, founded in reflective practice.

Examining how low-income female teachers enact agency has revealed a dichotomy of practice in which external authority and expectations are met within the classroom in contrast to the social realities outside the classroom. This duality reveals how teachers operate within a learning culture of external rules of affirmation and efficacy. They lack sufficient systems and structures to assess their own teaching, other than student exam performance and adhering to expected duties. This is based on a fundamental summative approach to learning, of the need to fill 'empty vessels' and draw on the authority of external experts that define what should be known.

Hence, teacher effectiveness is key to female teacher agency (see Table 5.1). It enables teachers to understand their roles based on the consequences and impact of what they do within the classroom, of their human action in relation to students and to support student learning through the distinct teacher–student relationship that brings together the maternal, professional and personal aspects of their social relation. In terms of low-income female teacher agency, this enables teachers to understand their roles through criteria that are open to them to construct even if it is to reproduce frames of authority and

Table 5.1: Teacher effectiveness to support female teacher agency

Understand roles based on what impact they have on student learning	What methods work for them and what is to be adjusted – ability to adapt expertise in the classroom and develop critical reflective analysis
Brings together maternal, professional and personal aspects of their relationships with students	Classroom space that supports female teachers to enact values that build relationships and supports professional development in practice
Individual ways students learn to build understanding of specific student needs and how to support them	Support students within their locality and school by considering the specific cohort in front of them

didactic learning. It opens the door towards evaluating practice and continual learning for teachers.

Knowing what works in their classroom brings immediate and specific benefits for students and teachers. Teachers can support students within their locality, school and community to flourish and thrive by focusing on students immediately in front of them. By learning from the idiosyncrasies of how their students learn, they can build their unique and individual understanding of the needs of a particular group of students and how to support their learning. They can learn what works for them and how teaching is to be adjusted. This can only work if teachers are supported to look beyond what is expected of them and their students to focus on the immediate needs of students in their classroom. For this, the classroom itself needs to be a distinct space that supports female teacher agency in which teachers enact values that build student relationships and develop pedagogical skills in practice.

Author reflections

I used convenience sampling to locate and access schools located in Lingarajapuram, North Bangalore. I grew up in Lingarajapuram for most of my childhood, before moving to live in the UK at the age of 12. I have returned every year since and continue to have close involvement and links to this part of Bangalore. It is where I chose to conduct my research as it is the area I am personally invested in and a distinct part of my identity. Despite my familiarity with the local area, I was advised by local connections that an initial introduction made by a mutual connection should be made to schools in the area. This was to mitigate any hesitancy or suspicion of an unknown person to the institution, coming in and observing them. Although, hospitality and a culture of welcoming strangers are prevalent within Indian culture, a guest who is welcomed into one's home is distinct from an outsider who may scrutinise and evaluate one's institution. My motivations and intentions toward the school were crucial to receiving their participation. This itself was a process of negotiation where I navigated perceptions of myself and who I might represent. An intermediary was needed between me as outsider and the school management. Initial introductions were made with a mutual, trusted colleague that assured the school of my intentions, background, and ties to the local community. Having lived in Lingarajapuram and returning frequently worked partly in my favour to ensure that representation of the school would be tied to my representation as being from the same area.

Meetings between myself and the principal of each school took place in which their agreement to participate was given and teachers selected by the principal to take part in the research. Within these introductory meetings, I reiterated my personal commitment to the local community, emphasising my 'insider' status of being both Indian and that my family lived and worked in the local area. Once assured of my motivations, management were more open to discussing their school structure, asked questions about my education in the UK and discussed the state of education in India. This was an important stage in negotiations between me and the school, as conversation was critical to ensuring their participation and being able to conduct my research. Permission was based on the need for me to sit at management's desk and verbally request their participation. The conversation about who I was, and my education supported my request, but it appeared far more important that management's positional authority to me was acknowledged. This experience of navigating these social spaces served as a valuable introduction to what teachers later interviewed might face on an everyday basis. What was initially a set of barriers and hurdles proved to be critical in placing into context teachers' responses about their roles and perspectives on their teaching.

In terms of my development through this research, I found that a great deal of my assumptions regarding agency and the subjugated status of low-income Indian women were challenged and reshaped. Teacher responses acted as a foil to structural inequalities that I am embedded within and was unaware of, despite feeling that I rose above hierarchical assumptions in my researcher status. From attempts to secure school participation within Lingarajapuram, to analysing interview data, I have been increasingly reminded of my outsider role. Despite paying close attention to the speech of Amu, Deepa, Bhargavi and Celina, it is possible that in my outsider status, I have still not heard all that was said to me. Yet, it is this element of distance that I am thankful for. It has highlighted that frameworks and constructs placed upon the low-income Indian woman, however carefully analysed and mitigated for, cannot fully lay bare their private and personal thoughts and feelings.

I set out to examine the values of a group of low-income female teachers from low-income schools in Lingarajapuram, Bangalore, India. From approaching schools to participate, meeting teachers, and interviewing them through to written transcripts and analysis of their words, I was committed to the individual opinions, experiences, and lives of these teachers. Values gleaned from their words revealed insight into the lives and experiences of this group of teachers. There is no greater need for education reform in India than to support this demographic group in their professional development and understanding of their teaching practice. They have demonstrated deep commitment to their students and utilise what resources they have available to enable student achievement.

An understanding of social justice throughout this research indicated that it was far more complex than individual emancipation for people for whom emancipation is a clear and visible construct. Agency demonstrated by female teachers showed their skill developed at early childhood in navigating the many expectations and pressures they face. Yet these women work, care and still find emotional support for their students so burn-out is not an option for them. The mental health of these women is often not considered and is seen as of little importance in the wider context of social and economic emancipation. As a teacher, wife and mother myself, it is difficult not to help identify with these teachers in the expectations and demands placed on them, yet I have afforded to me greater degrees of freedom in my socio-economic status and privilege. Although I agree with Cochran-Smith's (2010) approach to social justice and very much take on the teacher as activist role within my own practice, it is something that cannot be easily engendered among marginalised groups as facilitated or directed by myself, nor should it be. I represent the oppressor role despite my beliefs that I am otherwise (Freire, 1996).

If social justice within teacher education promotes equality of opportunity, respect of groups and the teacher as activist (Cochran-Smith, 2010), teacher responses show social justice of this kind cannot be easily integrated among teachers who perpetuate such inequalities. Therefore, do we dismiss it and say it is impossible? Do we throw our hands up and say we cannot help them if they cannot help themselves? Perhaps, how these teachers have approached agency can help reveal new ways of understanding social justice as happening beneath the surface: of the teacher attempting to work within their restrictions and limitations, however implicit and tacit; of maintaining survival and managing roles while part of such structures through the careful negotiation of their speech. Does social justice action have to be front and centre, explicitly voicing and highlighting injustices? How do you navigate such injustices if they are part of your daily life?

Teachers' responses have revealed that low-income female teachers do not have the space to advocate for their students. They are not afforded the language, training and validation beyond their gendered role within the classroom. That does not mean they do not care for their students. It is that teaching is a matter of social and economic emancipation and not of dealing with social injustice. Social justice currently has no place in the Indian classroom: teachers' roles are to prepare students to raise themselves and their families out of poverty by being part of the very system that enacts such inequalities. Emancipatory objectives are fundamental for teachers to be activists. However, within the Indian classroom this is defined by a neoliberal emphasis on education as a gateway to financial stability and not the space or place for teachers to question or critique inequalities.

Throughout this research, I became used to finding ideological blocks, or instances where I felt a certain perspective or approach just would not fit within the Indian context of education. Far from being a negative experience, it forced me to focus away from solutions or ways to fix a problem. Instead, as with the teachers I interviewed, it led me to work around the rigidity or inapplicability of constructs toward negotiation; toward re-envisioning social justice as that which is hidden beneath the surface, working in the background towards low-income female teacher survival and place within their personal and professional lives.

References

Ajmer University (no date) *Syllabus for four year integrated*. Available at: https://www.mdsuajmer.ac.in/syllabus/169_201516_SYL_BABED_RIE.pdf

Åkerlind, G.S. (2012) 'Variation and commonality in phenomenographic research methods', *Higher Education Research & Development*, 31(1), pp 115–27. Available at: https://doi.org/10.1080/07294360.2011.642845.

Akkerman, S.F. and Meijer, P.C. (2011) 'A dialogical approach to conceptualizing teacher identity', *Teaching and Teacher Education*, 27(2), pp 308–19. Available at: https://doi.org/10.1016/j.tate.2010.08.013.

Alam, S. and Debnath, S. (2022) 'Future of teacher education in the context of NEP 2020', *International Journal of Latest Research in Humanities and Social Science*, 5(10), pp 17–20. Available at: http://www.ijlrhss.com/paper/volume-5-issue-10/3-HSS-1480.pdf

Anand, S. and Sen, A. (2000) 'Human development and economic sustainability', *World Development*, 28(12), pp 2029–49. Available at: https://doi.org/10.1016/S0305-750X(00)00071-1.

Basu, A. (2010) 'Who secures women's capabilities in Martha Nussbaum's quest for social justice?', *Columbia Journal of Gender and Law*, 19(1), pp 201–18.

Batra, P. (2014) 'Problematising teacher education practice in India: Developing a research agenda', *Education as Change*, 18(1), pp S5–S18. Available at: https://doi.org/10.1080/16823206.2013.877358.

Bergman, R. (2004) 'Caring for the ethical ideal: Nel Noddings on moral education', *Journal of Moral Education*, 33(2), pp 149–62. Available at: https://doi.org/10.1080/0305724042000215203.

Berliner, D.C. (2001) 'Learning about and learning from expert teachers', *International Journal of Educational Research*, 35(5), pp 463–82. Available at: https://doi.org/10.1016/S0883-0355(02)00004-6.

Biggs, J. (1996) 'Enhancing teaching through constructive alignment', *Higher Education*, 32(3), pp 347–64. Available at: https://doi.org/10.1007/BF00138871.

Brady, L. (2011) 'Teacher values and relationship: Factors in values education', *Australian Journal of Teacher Education*, 36(2), pp 56–66. Available at: https://doi.org/10.14221/ajte.2011v36n2.5.

Burkitt, I. (2016) 'Relational agency', *European Journal of Social Theory*, 19(3), pp 322–39. Available at: https://doi.org/10.1177/1368431015591426.

Busby, C. (1999) 'Agency, power and personhood: Discourses of gender and violence in a fishing community in south India', *Critique of Anthropology*, 19(3), pp 227–48. Available at: https://doi.org/10.1177/0308275X9901900302.

Campbell, R.J., Kyriakides, L., Muijs, D. and Robinson, W. (2004) 'Effective teaching and values: Some implications for research and teacher appraisal', *Oxford Review of Education*, 30(4), pp 451–65. Available at: https://doi.org/Doi 10.1080/0305498042000303955.

Carr, D. (2005) 'Personal and interpersonal relationships in education and teaching: A virtue ethical perspective', *British Journal of Educational Studies*, 53(3), pp 37–41. Available at: https://doi.org/10.1111/j.1467-8527.2005.00294.x.

Carr, D. (2006) 'Professional and personal values and virtues in education and teaching', *Oxford Review of Education*, 32(2), pp 171–83. Available at: https://doi.org/10.1080/03054980600645354.

Chaturvedi, A., Chiu, C.-Y. and Viswanathan, M. (2009) 'Literacy, negotiable fate, and thinking style among low income women in India', *Journal of Cross-Cultural Psychology*, 40(5), pp 880–93. Available at: https://doi.org/10.1177/0022022109339391.

Clarke, P. (2001) *Teaching and Learning: The Culture of Pedagogy*. New Delhi: SAGE.

Clegg, J.W. (2011) 'The ontological commitments of relational philosophy', *Journal of Constructivist Psychology*, 24(4), pp 324–327. Available at: https://doi.org/10.1080/10720537.2011.593473.

Cochran-Smith, M. (2010) 'Toward a theory of teacher education for social justice', in A. Hargreaves, A. Lieberman, M. Fullan and D. Hopkins (eds) *Second International Handbook of Educational Change*. London and New York: Springer, pp 445–68.

Cohen, L., Manion, L. and Morrison, K. (2007) *Research Methods in Education*. Oxford: Routledge.

Creswell, J.W. and Miller, D.L. (2000) 'Determining validity in qualitative inquiry', *Theory into Practice*, 39(3), pp 125–30.

Crocker, D.A. (1992) 'Functioning and capability: The foundations of Sen's and Nussbaum's development ethic', *Political Theory*, 20(4), pp 584–612.

Cunliffe, A.L. (2009) 'The philosopher leader: On relationalism, ethics and reflexivity – A critical perspective', *Management Learning*, 40(1), pp 87–101. Available at: https://doi.org/10.1177/1350507608099315.

De Herdt, T. and Bastiaensen, J. (2008) 'The circumstances of agency', *International Development Review*, 30(4), pp 339–58.

Department of Education (2019) *Four Year Integrated B.Sc.B.Ed. Programme*. Napaam. Available at: https://www.tezu.ernet.in/dedu/syllabus/2021/LOCF%20Int_B.Sc.B.Ed.pdf

Dewey, J. (2011) *Democracy and Education*. LaVerge, TN: Simon and Brown.

Dill, J.S. (2007) 'Durkheim and Dewey and the challenge of contemporary moral education', *Journal of Moral Education*, 36(2), pp 221–37. Available at: https://doi.org/10.1080/03057240701325357.

Dyer, C., Choksi, A., Awasty, V., Iyer, U., Moyade, R., Nigam, N. et al (2002) 'Democratising teacher education research in India', *Comparative Education*, 38(3), pp 337–51. Available at: https://doi.org/10.1080/0305006022000014197.

Dyer, C., Choksi, A., Awasty, V., Iyer, U., Moyade, R., Nigam, N. et al (2004) 'Knowledge for teacher development in India: The importance of "local knowledge" for in-service education', *International Journal of Educational Development*, 24(1), pp 39–52. Available at: https://doi.org/10.1016/j.ijedudev.2003.09.003.

Feldman, S. and Gellert, P. (2006) 'The seductive quality of central human capabilities: Sociological insights into Nussbaum and Sen's disagreement', *Economy and Society*, 35(3), pp 423–52. Available at: https://doi.org/10.1080/03085140600845008.

Freire, P. (1996) *Pedagogy of the Oppressed*. London: Penguin.

Fox, C. (2008) 'Postcolonial dilemmas in narrative research', *Compare*, 38(3), pp 335–47. Available at: https://doi.org/10.1080/03057920802066634.

Ganapathy-Coleman, H. (2014) '"Teachers are always good. Children have flaws": Memories of school and learning in the narratives of low-income parents in India', *Psychology and Developing Societies*, 26(1), pp 29–58. Available at: https://doi.org/10.1177/0971333613516227.

Gee, J.P. (2005) *An Introduction to Discourse Analysis Theory and Method*. Oxford: Taylor & Francis.

Gee, J.P. (2011) *How to do Discourse Analysis*. New York and London: Routledge.

Gee, J.P. and Green, J.L. (1998) 'Discourse analysis, learning, and social practice: A methodological study', *Review of Research in Education*, 23(1), 119–69.

Gergen, K.J. (2011) 'Relational being: A brief introduction', *Journal of Constructivist Psychology*, 24(4), pp 280–2. Available at: https://doi.org/10.1080/10720537.2011.593453.

Giddens, A. (1991) *Modernity and Self-Identity: Self and Society in the Late Modern Age*. Oxford: Blackwell Publishers Ltd.

Glassdoor (2023) *Glassdoor*. Available at: https://www.glassdoor.co.uk/Salaries/bangalore-software-engineer-salary-SRCH_IL.0,9_IM1091_KO10,27.htm

Gordon, M. (2009) 'The misuses and effective uses of constructivist teaching', *Teachers and Teaching: Theory and Practice*, 15(6), pp 737–46. Available at: https://doi.org/10.1080/13540600903357058.

Guba, E.G. and Lincoln, Y.S. (1994) 'Competing paradigms in qualitative research', in N.K. Denzin and Y.S. Lincoln (eds) *Handbook of Qualitative Research*. Thousand Oaks, CA: SAGE, pp 105–17.

Gupta, A. (2003) 'Socio-cultural-historical constructivism in the preparation and practice of early childhood teachers in New Delhi, India', *Journal of Early Childhood Teacher Education*, 24(3), pp 163–70. Available at: https://doi.org/10.1080/1090102030240305.

Gupta, B., Gupta, B.L. and Choubey, A.K. (2021) 'Higher education institutions: Some guidelines for obtaining and sustaining autonomy in the context of NEP 2020', *International Journal of All Research Education and Scientific Methods (IJARESM)*, 9(1). Available at: https://www.researchgate.net/publication/348408191_Higher_Education_Institutions_-Some_Guidelines_for_Obtaining_and_Sustaining_Autonomy_in_the_Context_of_Nep_2020

Hammersley, M. (2007) 'The issue of quality in qualitative research', *International Journal of Research & Method in Education*, 30(3), pp 287–305. Available at: https://doi.org/10.1080/17437270701614782.

Hargreaves, A. (1998) 'The emotional practice of teaching', *Teaching and Teacher Education*, 14(8), pp 835–54.

Hattie, J. (2003) 'Teachers make a difference: What is the research evidence?', *Lloydia Cincinnati*, 12, pp 1–17. Available at: http://www.annedavies.com/pdf/19C_expertteachers_hattie.pdf

Higgins, C. (2003) 'Teaching and the good life: A critique of the ascetic ideal in education', *Educational Theory*, 53(2), pp 9–12. Available at: https://doi.org/10.1111/j.1741-5446.2003.00131.x

Hodkinson, A. and Devarakonda, C. (2011) 'Conceptions of inclusion and inclusive education: A critical examination of the perspectives and practices of teachers in England', *British Education Studies Association*, 3(1), pp 52–65.

Honnashetty, S., Reddy, M. and Hanumanthappa, M. (2013) 'Phrase structure based English to Kannada sentence translation', *International Journal of Computer and Communication Technology*, 4(3), pp 25–29.

International Labour Organisation and UNESCO (2015) 'Changing employment relationships in the teaching profession', Bill Ratteree, background paper for discussion at the 12th Session of the CEART (Paris, 20–24 April). Geneva.

Jandhyala, K. and Ramachandran, V. (2009) 'Why women teachers matter in secondary education', *Economic and Political Weekly*, L(32), pp 48–54.

Joshi, A. (2009) 'What do teacher–child interactions in early childhood classrooms in India look like? Teachers' and parents' perspectives', *Early Child Development and Care*, 179(3), pp 285–301. Available at: https://doi.org/10.1080/03004430601078610.

Joshi, A. and Taylor, A. (2005) 'Perceptions of early childhood teachers and parents of teacher–parent interactions in an Indian context', *Early Child Development and Care*, 175(4), pp 343–59. Available at: https://doi.org/10.1080/0300443042000266213.

Kachru, B.B. (2016) 'The Indianness in Indian English', *Word*, 21(3), pp 391–410. Available at: https://doi.org/10.1080/00437956.1965.11435436.

King, G., Keohane, R.O. and Verba, S. (1994) *Designing Social Inquiry: Scientific Inference in Qualitative Research*. Princeton, NJ: Princeton University Press.

Klaassen, C.A. (2002) 'Teacher pedagogical competence and sensibility', *Teaching and Teacher Education*, 18(2), pp 151–8. Available at: https://doi.org/10.1016/S0742-051X(01)00060-9.

Kumar, G. and Pandey, J. (2012) 'How Indian and Western teacher trainees differ in their perception about values', *Journal of Human Values*, 18(1), pp 73–84. Available at: https://doi.org/10.1177/097168581101800106.

Kumar, K. (1988) 'Origins of India's "textbook culture"', *Comparative Education Review*, 32(4), pp 452–64.

Kumar, K. (2005) 'Quality of education at the beginning of the 21st century: Lessons from India', *Indian Educational Review*, 41(1), pp 4–28.

Kumar, K. (2010) 'Culture, state and girls: An educational perspective', *Economic and Political Weekly*, 45(17), pp 75–84. Available at: https://www.jstor.org/stable/25664388

Kumar, K. (2011) 'Teaching and the neo-liberal state', *Economic and Political Weekly*, 46(21), pp 37–40. Available at: https://www.jstor.org/stable/23017223

Lange, C. (2012) *The Syntax of Spoken Indian English*. Amsterdam: John Benjamins Publishing.

Lovat, T. (2011) 'Values education and holistic learning: Updated research perspectives', *International Journal of Educational Research*, 50(3), pp 148–52. Available at: https://doi.org/10.1016/j.ijer.2011.07.009.

Lovat, T. (2013) 'Jurgen Habermas: Education's reluctant hero', in M. Murphy (ed) *Social Theory and Education Research: Understanding Foucault, Habermas, Bourdieu and Derrida*. Abingdon: Routledge, pp 69–83.

Malterud, K. (2001) 'Qualitative research: Standards, challenges, and guidelines', *The Lancet*, 358(9280), pp 483–8.

Manjrekar, N. (2013) 'Women school teachers in new times: Some preliminary reflections', *Indian Journal of Gender Studies*, 20(2), pp 335–56. Available at: https://doi.org/10.1177/0971521513482223.

Maslak, M.A. and Singhal, G. (2008) 'The identity of educated women in India: confluence or divergence ?', *Gender and Education*, 20(5), pp 481–493. Available at: https://doi.org/10.1080/09540250701829961.

Menon, S., Viswanatha, V. and Sahi, J. (2014) 'Teaching in two tongues: Rethinking the role of language(s) in teacher education in India', *Contemporary Education Dialogue*, 11(1), pp 41–65. Available at: https://doi.org/10.1177/0973184913509752.

Mlecko, J.D. (1982) 'The Guru in Hindu tradition', *Numen*, 29, pp 33–61.

Mooij, J. (2008) 'Primary education, teachers' professionalism and social class about motivation and demotivation of government school teachers in India', *International Journal of Educational Development*, 28(5), pp 508–23. Available at: https://doi.org/10.1016/j.ijedudev.2007.10.006.

Morrow, V. (2013) 'Whose values? Young people's aspirations and experiences of schooling in Andhra Pradesh, India', *Children & Society*, 27(4), pp 258–69. Available at: https://doi.org/10.1111/chso.12036.

National Council of Educational Research and Training (2016) *Programme Syllabus for Bachelor of Education (B.Ed.) Programme*. New Delhi.

NEP (2020) *National Education Policy 2020*, Ministry of Human Resource Development, Government of India. Available at: www.education.gov.in/sites/upload_files/mhrd/files/NEP_Final_English_0.pdf

Noddings, N. (2003) 'Is teaching a practice?', *Journal of Philosophy of Education*, 37(2), pp 241–51. Available at: https://doi.org/10.1111/1467-9752.00323.

Nussbaum, M.C. (1999) 'Women and equality: The capabilities approach', *International Labour Review*, 138(3), pp 227–45.

Nussbaum, M.C. (2007) 'Human rights and human capabilities', *Harvard Human Rights Journal*, 20, pp 21–4.

Nussbaum, M.C. (2009) 'Creating capabilities: The human development approach and its implementation', *Transgender Studies and Feminism: Theory, Politics and Gendered Realities*, 24(3), pp 211–15.

Oser, F. (2013) 'Fritz Oser models of moral behaviour', in K. Heinrichs, F. Oser, and T. Lovat (eds) *Handbook of Moral Motivation: Theories, Models and Applications*. Rotterdam: Sense Publishers, pp 7–24.

Planning Commission Government of India (2015) *Number of teachers (Male/Female) in primary and upper primary school at all India level from year 2001 to 2010*, Open Government Data Platform India. Available at: https://visualize.data.gov.in/?inst=b10599c5-4f2f-4001-8f21-cbb1e3ca4b85

Prickett, S. (2007) 'Guru or teacher? Shishya or student? Pedagogic shifts in South Asian dance training in India and Britain', *South Asia Research*, 27(1), pp 25–41. Available at: https://doi.org/10.1177/026272800602700102.

Prosser, M. and Trigwell, K. (1997) 'Using phenomenography in the design of programs for teachers in higher education', *Higher Education Research & Development*, 16(2), pp 41–54. Available at: https://doi.org/10.1080/0729436970160104.

Ramachandran, V. (2000) 'Education and the status of women', in V. Ramachandran (ed) *Paper prepared for EFA 2000 Assessment Indian National Commission for Co-operation with UNESCO Department of Education, MHRD, Government of India*. Jaipur: Educational Resource Unit, pp 1–34.

Ramachandran, V. (2003) *Gender Equality in Education in India*. Available at: https://www.researchgate.net/publication/239600209

Richardson, V. (2003) 'Constructivist pedagogy', *Teachers College Record*, 105(9), pp 1623–40. Available at: https://doi.org/10.1046/j.1467-9620.2003.00303.x.

Rizvi, F., Lingard, B. and Lavia, J. (2006) 'Postcolonialism and education: Negotiating a contested terrain', *Pedagogy, Culture & Society*, 14(3), pp 249–62. Available at: https://doi.org/10.1080/14681360600891852.

Robinson-Pant, A. and Singal, N. (2013a) 'Research ethics in comparative and international education: Reflections from anthropology and health', *Compare: A Journal of Comparative and International Education*, 43(4), pp 443–64. Available at: https://doi.org/10.1080/03057925.2013.797725.

Robinson-Pant, A. and Singal, N. (2013b) 'Researching ethically across cultures: Issues of knowledge, power and voice', *Compare: A Journal of Comparative and International Education*, 43(4), pp 417–21. Available at: https://doi.org/10.1080/03057925.2013.797719.

Sanghani, R. (2015) 'The uncomfortable truth about racism and the suffragettes', *The Telegraph*, 6 October. Available at: https://www.telegraph.co.uk/women/womens-life/11914757/Racism-and-the-suffragettes-the-uncomfortable-truth.html

Sarangapani, P.M. (2003) 'Childhood and schooling in an Indian village', *Childhood*, 10(4), pp 403–18. Available at: https://doi.org/10.1177/0907568203104002.

Sen, A. (1997) 'Editorial: Human capital and human capability', *World Development*, 25(12), pp 1959–61. Available at: https://doi.org/10.1016/S0305-750X(97)10014-6.

Sen, A. (2005) 'Human rights and capabilities', *Journal of Human Development*, 6(2), pp 151–66. Available at: https://doi.org/10.1080/14649880500120491.

Singal, N. (2005) 'Mapping the field of inclusive education: A review of the Indian literature', *International Journal of Inclusive Education*, 9(4), pp 331–50. Available at: https://doi.org/10.1080/13603110500138277.

Singal, N. (2006) 'Inclusive education in India: International concept, national interpretation', *International Journal of Disability, Development and Education*, 53(3), pp 351–69. Available at: https://doi.org/10.1080/10349120600847797.

Singh Dhillon, S. and Bharti, A. (no date) 'Blending of ICT: Restructuring of teacher education', *Shodha Prabha (UGC CARE Journal)*, 47(8), p 2022.

Smail, A. (2013) 'Rediscovering the teacher within Indian child-centred pedagogy: Implications for the global Child-Centred Approach', *Compare: A Journal of Comparative and International Education*, 44(4), pp 613–33. Available at: https://doi.org/10.1080/03057925.2013.817225.

Spivak, G.C. (2005) 'Scattered speculations on the subaltern and the popular', *Postcolonial Studies: Culture, Politics, Economy*, 8(4), pp 475–86. Available at: https://doi.org/10.1080/13688790500375132.

Sridhar, S.N. (1992) 'The ecology of bilingual competence: language interaction in the syntax of indigenized varieties of English', I(2), pp 141–50.

Sriprakash, A. (2011) 'Being a teacher in contexts of change: Education reform and the repositioning of teachers' work in India', *Contemporary Education Dialogue*, 8(1), pp 5–31. Available at: https://doi.org/10.1177/097318491000800102.

State Government of Karnataka (2022a) *41 Hospitals and Nursing Homes*. Available at: https://karmikaspandana.karnataka.gov.in/storage/pdf-files/minimum%20wages/HOSPITALS%20%20AND%20NURSHING%20HOMES.pdf

State Government of Karnataka (2022b) *5780 Employment in Residential Houses including Domestic Helpers, Child Care Assistants, Home Nurses and Allied Domestic Works*. Available at: https://karmikaspandana.karnataka.gov.in/storage/pdf-files/mwnew/domestic.pdf

Sugarman, J. and Martin, J. (2011) 'Theorizing relational agency: Reactions to comments', *Journal of Constructivist Psychology*, 24(4), pp 321–3. Available at: https://doi.org/10.1080/10720537.2011.593472.

Thirumurthy, V., Szecsi, T., Hardin, B.J. and Koo, R.D. (2007) 'Honoring teachers: A world of perspectives', *Journal of Early Childhood Teacher Education*, 28(2), pp 181–98. Available at: https://doi.org/10.1080/10901020701366764.

Thornberg, R. (2008) 'The lack of professional knowledge in values education', *Teaching and Teacher Education*, 24(7), pp 1791–8. Available at: https://doi.org/10.1016/j.tate.2008.04.004.

Tight, M. (2016) 'Phenomenography: The development and application of an innovative research design in higher education research', *International Journal of Social Research Methodology*, 5579(February), pp 319–38. Available at: https://doi.org/10.1080/13645579.2015.1010284.

Triveni, S. (2014) 'Value orientation of college teachers', *Indian Journal of Health and Wellbeing*, 5(10), pp 1156–60.

UNESCO and Ministry of Education and Science Spain (1994) *The Salamanca Statement and Framework for Action on Special Needs Education, World Conference on Special Needs Education: Access and Quality*. Salamanca.

Unified District Information System for Education (2014) *State-wise Percentage of Schools With Female Teachers – DISE 2012–13: Flash Statistics, Open Government Data Platform India*. Available at: https://visualize.data.gov.in/?inst=d86b89d7-3799-4456-86da-9756ccd1ab01

Vijaysimha, I. (2013) '"We are Textbook Badnekais!": A Bernsteinian analysis of textbook culture in science classrooms', *Contemporary Education Dialogue*, 10(1), pp 67–97. Available at: https://doi.org/10.1177/0973184912465161.

White, B.C. (2002) 'Constructing constructivist teaching: Reflection as research', *Reflective Practice*, 3(3), pp 307–26. Available at: https://doi.org/10.1080/1462394022000034550.

Willig, C. (2014) 'Discourses and discourse analysis', in U. Flick (ed) *The SAGE Handbook of Qualitative Data Analysis*. Thousand Oaks, CA: SAGE, pp 341–53.

World Bank (2019a) *Gender Data Portal World Bank Economic Opportunities, World Bank*. Available at: http://datatopics.worldbank.org/gender/country/india

World Bank (2019b) *Gender Indicators Report, World Bank*. Available at: https://databank.worldbank.org/indicator/SL.TLF.TOTL.FE.ZS?id=2ddc971b&report_name=Gender_Indicators_Report&populartype=series#

Zembylas, M. (2005) 'Discursive practices, genealogies, and emotional rules: A poststructuralist view on emotion and identity in teaching', *Teaching and Teacher Education*, 21(8), pp 935–48. Available at: https://doi.org/10.1016/j.tate.2005.06.005.

Index

A

access
  concept of 3–4
  to higher education 15
  to quality education 16–17
achievement 62, 127–8
  academic 13, 59–61, 111, 128, 131
  collective 61
  communal 64
  sense of 111–16
  and transformation, as act of teacher creativity 121–3
act of giving, teaching as an 35–6
active learning 20, 136
actual freedom 12, 59, 60
additional duties, lack of compensation for 12
administrative responsibilities and duties 10, 12, 13
agency 12, 116, 145
  and autonomy 9
  explicit and visible 139–49
  linguistic negotiation as acts of relational 97–8
  within teacher roles, social spaces and attitudes to transformation 126
  teachers' sense of 42
  through determining place among others 125
  through speech in navigating social spaces 127
  through transformative action on others 127
  voice as 95–8
agricultural labour 3
Ajmer University 19
Åkerlind, G.S. 26
Akkerman, S.F. 138
Andhra Pradesh 13, 46, 62
Aristotle 42
assertive positioning 89, 91, 127
authenticity
  cultural 53
  of knowledge 36, 101–2, 104–18, 107, 119, 122–3, 127
  of living 44
  morality of 43–4, 62–3, 119–20
authoritative knowledge 36, 123, 131, 141
authority, of teacher 24, 52, 120, 123
avocation of the relational being 96, 98

B

Bangalore 16, 26–7
BEd programmes 14–20, 21, 28, 121, 136, 141

beliefs 30, 36, 43, 44, 50, 53, 78, 121
Biggs, J. 135
builder, teacher's role as 102, 121–2, 128
Burkitt, I. 94–5
Busby, C. 2

C

capability approach 10, 12, 127
  see also central human capabilities (CHC)
capability ethic 10
care and caring 52, 64, 117, 129–30, 138, 147
Carr, D. 42–3, 117, 122
caste system 27, 39, 51, 53, 121
central human capabilities (CHC) 10–11, 61, 78, 80, 82
centralised examinations 8
certificate programme 18
character education ideal 42–3
child marriage 4
child-centred policies 9–10, 34, 133, 135, 141
Clarke, P. 139
classroom, and female teacher empowerment 128–32
Cochran-Smith, M. 137–8, 145
cognitive development 37
collective emancipation 62, 63, 64
collective identity 77, 97, 98, 127, 129
collective strengths 19
colonialism, impact on education 4, 8, 51, 133
commodification
  of education 6
  of women 3
communal identity 73, 77
conflict 86, 99
  avoidance 77–8, 82, 85, 86, 99–100, 121–2
  social significance 14
  teacher views on 82–4
  traditional and cultural significance 13, 14
constructivism 19–20, 123, 134, 135–6, 142
contract teachers 5
control, concept of 3–4
convenience, of being a teacher 75–6
Creswell, J.W. 103
critical self-reflexivity 105–6, 119
criticisms, impact of 81–2
cultural authenticity 53
cultural inequalities 1–2

cultural models 139
Cunliffe, A.L. 105

D

defensive positioning 85, 89, 91, 93, 127
Delhi Declaration for Education for All, 1994 9
demotivation 12, 13, 51
description and narrative, in disseminating knowledge 120–1
devotion, of students 33, 49, 50, 113
Dewey, J. 36, 37, 42, 119
dignity 3, 13, 14
Dill, J.S. 36, 42
diploma programme 18
disciplining 39, 41, 42, 58, 78, 84, 92–3, 115, 117
discourse analysis 29
disruptive students 41
distributed personhood of knowledge 102, 119–20, 121, 122–3
domestic duties 4, 129
domestic violence 2
Durkheim, E. 36, 37, 42
duty of care 63, 64, 65
  see also care and caring
Dyer, C. 20–1

E

Early Childhood Care and Education (ECCE) 18
education
  as a commodity 12, 59
  policies 132
    child-centred 9–10, 34, 133, 135, 141
    historic, impact of 7–9
    neoliberal 10, 52, 146
    reform 6
    significance of 10–11
elliptical repetition 31, 68, 69, 72, 73
emancipation 43, 50, 63, 145
  collective 62, 63, 64
  economic 63
  and freedom of choice 43–5
  social 63
emotional relationships 136, 137
employment objective 11, 13, 109–10, 132
English language 130
  as a space for agency 86–9
  internal and external social spaces 91–4
  used as underlying values of representation 89–91
ethics, professional 42–3

F

family obligations 2, 15, 46–8, 56
family support 54–5
Feldman, S. 11, 48, 53

female agency 6–7
  see also agency
female teacher identity 132, 138
freedom of choice 43, 44, 54, 98, 109, 142
Freire, P. 23, 50, 105, 122
functionalism 43

G

Ganapathy-Coleman, H. 53
Gee, J.P. 30, 67
Gellert, P. 11, 48, 53
gender 53, 77
  equality within education 4
  role in personal and professional aspirations 54–9
gendered qualities 58
gendered roles 54, 55, 59, 146
gendered spaces
  mediating through group consensus 69–75
  socially accepted spaces 75–7
Gergen, K.J. 96, 98
Giddens, A. 43–4, 62–3, 119
girls, education and childhood of 3–4
globalisation 6, 51
Gordon, M. 135
gratitude 50, 63, 64, 112, 116, 141
  reciprocal 54, 113, 114–15
  verbal 111–12, 113
group action 74
group identity 73
guide, teacher's role as 52
Gupta, A. 57
guru, teacher as 51
guru–shishya model 25, 51–4, 119, 120–1
  see also teacher–student relationships

H

Habermas, J. 104–6, 107, 119
Hammersley, M. 103
happiness 11, 78–9, 82, 128
hared suggestions 73
Hargreaves, A. 136–7
Hattie, J. 134–5
Higgins, C. 117
higher marks, emphasis on 108–9
historic education system and policies, impact of 7–9
historical inequalities 1–2
honesty 81
human capability *see* capability approach
human development paradigm 10, 61
  see also capability approach
husband, family of 17

I

immigrant communities from neighbouring states 82–3, 131
income, lack of control over 3

independent thinking 18, 122, 131
interfering, impact of 81–2
internal and external social spaces, of teachers 91–4
intonation 66, 68, 70, 71
I-positions 138, 140

K

Kannada 90
Karnataka 5, 16
Kerala, fishing community 2
Klaassen, C.A. 44
knowledge 134
  authentic 36, 101–2, 104–18, 107, 119, 122–3, 127
  authoritative 36, 123, 131, 141
  distributed personhood of 102, 119–20, 121, 122–3
  external sources of 36
  learning as acquisition of 48–9
  production and transformation 118–20
    dissemination of, description and narrative in 120–1
    and student achievement, as act of teacher creativity 121–3
  shared ownership, and academic achievement 59–61
  sharing 72
Kohlberg, L. 37
Kumar, G. 51
Kumar, K. 4, 8, 10, 35

L

Lange, C. 31
languages 130
  social 67–9
  see also English language
last bench students 41
learning as acquiring knowledge 48–9
learning culture 131, 132, 142
left dislocation 37–8
life politics 43–4, 62
linguistic negotiation 91, 97, 98, 127, 129
local government inspection of schools 12
Lovat, T. 36

M

Manjrekar, N. 6
marks-oriented approach 108–9
marriage 2, 4, 13, 54–7
Maslak, M.A. 2
maternal role 35, 57–8, 76, 96, 106, 137
meaningful life for teachers 12, 13, 53, 77, 79, 82, 85–6, 128
Meijer, P.C. 138, 139
menstruation 4
Miller, D.L. 103
misbehaving students 40–1

money, emphasis on 110
moral education 44, 86, 128, 129
moral purpose of education 36
morality of authenticity 43–4, 62–3, 119–20
Morrow, V. 13, 46, 59, 62
motivations 124, 139
  moral purpose of education 36–7
  reasons to become a teacher 32–6
mutual obligations 14

N

National Council for Education, Research and Training (NCERT) 8, 18
National Education Policy 1, 14–21
negotiation 7
  of personal contexts in teacher aspirations 45
  of professional contexts in teacher aspirations 48–50
neoliberal education policies 10–14, 52, 146
Netherlands, the 44
Noddings, N. 117
non-specific references 85, 89–90, 92, 93, 94
Nussbaum, M. 10, 11, 61, 142

O

ownership of land and commodities, denied access to 3

P

Pandey, J. 51
parents 115
  disrespect from 82–3
  influence of 50
passive actions 48
peace of mind 79–81, 82
perceptions of female work in India 55
performative action 39–40, 42
performative relationships 42
personal moral codes 42
personal virtues 43
Persons with Disability Act, 1995 9
phenomenography 26
phronesis 42, 43, 122
pillar, teacher's role as 86
pitch-glide 68
positional authority 24, 39, 40, 41–2, 86, 96, 101, 115–16, 123, 125, 128–30
poststructuralism 43
power relations, and its impact on emotions 137
powerlessness, female 3
private tutors 32
professional ethics 42–3
professional persona 19, 57, 58

Index

Q
questioning, to check student learning 41

R
Ramachandran, V. 3, 5–6, 55, 129
ranking system 108–9
rape cases 84, 131
reciprocal duty of care 63
reflective practice 19, 21, 104, 105, 122, 123, 133–4, 139
  implication for 65–6, 98–100
  need for reworking 141–3
  social relationships
    and implication for reflective practice 65–6
    and teachers' perceptions 63–5
  teacher effectiveness
    as emotional investment 136–7
    explicit and visible agency 139–40
    as social justice action 137–9
    as teacher expertise 134–6
  theory of 20
relational agency 94–5, 97–8, 103, 125, 129
relationship among teachers 72
religious beliefs 50
representation 7, 93–4, 97, 99
  collective 98–9
  in examining shared values of teachers 22–4
right dislocation 37–8
rote learning models 8, 9, 21

S
Salamanca Statement 9
Sarada Act 4
sati practice 4
satisfaction, sense of 81
scholarships 16–17
school and office environment, difference between 76
secondary teachers 5
self
  sense of 128–9, 138
  tacit negotiation of 140
self-denial 4
self-discovery 44, 63
self-efficacy 122
self-employment 111
self-examination 24
self-improvement 117–18
self-interest 118
selfless care 117
self-narratives 138–9
self-reflexivity 24, 105, 119
self-representation 23, 99
Sen, A. 10, 12–14, 59, 61, 142
shared values 14, 37
Singhal, G. 2
situated meaning 67–9
social interdependence 14
social justice 36, 137–9, 145–6
social models 139
social praxis 104, 107, 108
social relationships 29, 39, 48, 65, 125
  and implications for reflective practice 65–6
  and teachers' perceptions 63–5
social reproduction 6
social spaces 77–82
  basis of a meaningful life for teachers 85–6
  for female teachers 75–7
  teacher views on conflict 82–4
social status 9
societal obligations 13–14, 15
speech 38–9, 124, 130, 140
  linguistic negotiation, as acts of agency 97–8
  and space and relational agency 94–5
  voice as agency 95–8
  syntax and intonation of 68, 70–1
Spivak, G. 5, 6–7, 23, 97–9
standardised tests 13
student affirmation and acknowledgement, significance of 61, 117–18
student contribution 40
student failure 59–60, 64
  impact on teachers 60–1
student-teachers 19
study supplements and guides 83
subject knowledge, of teachers 136
summative learning model 20, 21
Sweden 44
synecdoche 97, 99
syntax 68
syntax intonation data analysis matrix 70–1

T
talent, significance of 109
teacher action, as group action 74
teacher affirmation on freedom of choice, impact of 116–18
teacher education 17
  programmes 65, 141
  reform 141
teacher effectiveness 137, 139, 142–3
  as emotional investment 136–7
  as social justice action 137–9
  as teacher expertise 134–6
teacher expertise 134–5
teacher identity 50, 139
teacher training 5, 15, 18, 21, 99, 124

teacher views
  on conflict 82–4
  of their sense of achievement 111–16
teacher–disciple relationships *see* guru–shishya model
teacher–student relationships 7, 35, 37–42, 106, 117, 142
  character education ideal 42–3
  emancipation and freedom of choice 43–5
  mutuality of purpose 44–5
  power dynamics 136
  see also guru–shishya model
teaching values 122
techne 42
textbooks 7–8, 118–19, 123–4, 127, 134
Thornberg, R. 44
topicalisation 68
transformation, attitudes to 102, 123
truth, value of 81
tuitions 33

V

value commodity 35
values 24, 36, 43, 64
  education 51
  impact of context and environment on 43
verbal speech 95
Vijaysimha, I. 118–19
violence, domestic 2
voice 66, 68, 101
  as agency for the female teacher 95–8

W

wage and salaried workers, among women 5
White, B.C. 140
Willig, C. 30

Y

'Young Lives Project' 13

Z

Zembylas, M. 136–7

www.ingramcontent.com/pod-product-compliance
Lightning Source LLC
Chambersburg PA
CBHW071709020426
42333CB00017B/2195